HOW DOES SHE DO IT?

Also by Paris Fury

Love & Fury: The Magic and Mayhem of Life with Tyson

HOW DOES SHE DO IT?

The Kids, Tyson & Me

PARIS FURY

HODDER &
STOUGHTON

First published in Great Britain in 2023 by Hodder & Stoughton
An Hachette UK company

7

Copyright © Paris Fury 2023

The right of Paris Fury to be identified as the Author of
the Work has been asserted by her in accordance with
the Copyright, Designs and Patents Act 1988.

A CIP catalogue record for this title is available from the British Library

Hardback ISBN 9781399710930
Trade Paperback ISBN 9781399710893
ebook ISBN 9781399710916

Typeset in Celeste by Hewer Text UK Ltd, Edinburgh
Printed and bound in Great Britain by Clays Ltd, Elcograf S.p.A.

Hodder & Stoughton policy is to use papers that are natural, renewable
and recyclable products and made from wood grown in sustainable
forests. The logging and manufacturing processes are expected to
conform to the environmental regulations of the country of origin.

Hodder & Stoughton Ltd
Carmelite House
50 Victoria Embankment
London EC4Y 0DZ

www.hodder.co.uk

CONTENTS

To my husband and children for helping me become the strong woman I feel I am today. And to my mother for putting the building blocks in place for me.

PROLOGUE

As the wife of a world champion boxer, the mother of an ever-growing family and the organiser of a mad busy household, there's one question I'm asked more than any other: 'How do you do it, Paris?'

So I've written this book to answer that very question. By offering a window into my hectic world, I'll reveal how I cope with the ups and downs of family life, whether that's facing tricky problems that test my strength and patience, or celebrating special milestones that make all the hard work worthwhile. I'll uncover the secrets of my happy marriage to Tyson – nearly fifteen years and counting – as well as the steps I take to look after my own health and well-being. And I'll also share the parenting tips and housekeeping hacks that keep my daily routine running as smoothly as possible.

I'm not going to pretend to be a flawless role model. I don't think the perfect wife and mother exists, to be honest. I'm the first to admit that I sometimes get it wrong, despite my best intentions, and have come to realise that the best way to learn is often through my mistakes. You won't find me suggesting that my approach to family life should be treated as gospel either, nor that it ought to be followed by everybody else. I totally respect that what works for me might not work for you. No one knows their home or their loved ones better than *you*, after all, and the last thing I want to do is preach or lecture. Just because I prefer my house full of hustle and bustle and comings and goings doesn't mean that you will too!

But I do hope, more than anything, that by sharing my know-how as a wife and a mother – with her own hopes and ambitions – I can offer support and encouragement to others. I realise how tough and challenging family life can be, yet experience has taught me to trust in my own instincts, to have faith in my own ability and, most importantly, to be kind to myself. I know only too well that there'll be good days and bad days, triumphs and traumas, and I try not to pile too much pressure on myself if things go wrong. I can only do my best.

But when all is said and done, my home and my family is at the heart of everything I do. In my eyes there's nothing more important than being a loyal wife and a good mother, and I work really hard to ensure that Tyson and the kids are properly looked after. Their welfare and well-being matters more to me than anything else on earth – if they're happy, I'm happy – so I gladly devote the lion's share of my time to those priorities. I learned these core family values in my Traveller childhood and sticking by them (and passing them down to my own children) means a great deal to me. I'm very proud of my heritage.

So anyone assuming that my life is non-stop glitz and glamour would be sorely mistaken. Away from the ring-side seats and the post-fight parties, I'm a busy, hands-on parent with children to raise and a household to manage. In common with most women in the Traveller community, I do my utmost to have a clean and clutter-free home – even though youngsters running around the place make this a challenge. In fact, I'm much more likely to be found whizzing a mop around the kitchen floor than enjoying a glass of rosé in a swanky bar. Only when the housework is completed, and my home is looking spotless, will I even consider a trip into town or beyond. I can't rest until everything is shipshape.

Tyson's frequent attendance at training camps also means I'm often left alone to keep house. Sometimes my husband can be absent for weeks on end – it's just part of the job – and after a while I'll find myself counting down the days on my calendar, desperate for my wingman to return home and give me a break. But, as with most aspects of my life, I'm used to rolling up my sleeves, knuckling down and getting things done. This positive and practical streak has been with me since childhood – Mam always taught me to be a 'can-do' person rather than a 'can't do' – and I've never let anyone or anything slow me down or hold me back. Keep calm and carry on, as they say.

For me, motherhood is the best job in the world but I'll never deny it's difficult. Like many women, I'm a plate-spinning, chore-juggling multitasker who spends half her time firefighting and troubleshooting, whether it's dealing with my baby's fussy eating, coping with my toddler's temper tantrums or confiscating my teenager's mobile phone. But, for all its hardships, bringing up children can also be an incredibly joyful and rewarding experience – if it wasn't, perhaps I wouldn't have decided to have so many! Every day can be chaos with such a big brood to look after, but I wouldn't change it for the world.

* * *

Anyone familiar with my story – maybe from our TV documentaries or my Instagram timeline – will know my family life hasn't always been plain sailing. My personal journey has witnessed many twists and turns that have tested my strength, my resilience and even my relationship. But it's these challenges and curveballs that have made me stop, think and realise what matters most in life. That was never more true than in August 2021, shortly after Athena was born, when my world suddenly came crashing down. Even now, I still shudder at the memory.

The birth had gone as well as expected – my daughter had weighed in at a healthy six pounds ten ounces, at the Royal Lancaster Infirmary – and Tyson and I were thrilled to bits with our new arrival. We now had three girls and three boys – what could be more perfect? – and couldn't wait to bring our beautiful baby home to meet her siblings. Tyson planned to spend the next fortnight with us before flying off to America to join his training camp, prior to his third title fight against Deontay Wilder.

But just a couple of hours after the delivery, we realised something was badly wrong. During a routine check, the midwife noticed Athena was breathing strangely and called the doctor over. He quickly pinpointed a racing heart rate – it was abnormally high, at over 300 beats per minute – and I could tell by his anxious expression that this was serious.

'Her heart's over-working, and we're worried this might badly affect her oxygen levels,' he said, as I descended into panic mode. 'We'll try our best to regulate things.'

Attempts to slow down Athena's heartbeat didn't have the desired effect, sadly, so a swift decision was made to blue-light her to Alder Hey children's hospital in Liverpool for specialist emergency treatment. Unable to travel in the ambulance, Tyson and I had to trail behind in the car. As we sped along the motorway I was barely able to speak. I was still light-headed from the epidural and was also in complete and utter shock. It felt so frightening being separated from my baby, only hours after her birth, and I was terrified she'd take a turn for the worse during the journey. I just wanted to be with her. My maternal instincts had kicked in massively.

When we finally arrived at Alder Hey I felt so weak and woozy that Tyson had to push me down the corridors in a wheelchair. We followed Athena as she was whisked off to the neonatal intensive care unit, where she was sedated, ventilated and placed into an incubator. She was quickly diagnosed with a condition called supraventricular tachycardia – SVT – and we were told she'd have to remain in ICU so the medical team could monitor her closely. It was clear that Athena was having the fight of her life, and that any deterioration might cause her to slip away at any moment.

* * *

What followed was the most traumatic fortnight I've ever known. It was a living nightmare. I consider myself an emotionally strong person – I'm the latest in a long line of tough Traveller women – but never before had I felt so fragile and helpless. I sat beside the incubator for hours on end, praying to God ('Dear Lord, please save my precious girl . . .') as I watched my daughter's tiny chest rise and fall in rhythm with the ventilator. Not only was I worried sick about Athena, my heart ached for my five other children in Morecambe who, although well cared for by their granny, were upset and bewildered that Mam and the baby hadn't yet come home. I missed them so much, and only wished I could be in two places at once.

While Athena was in the ICU, Tyson and I stayed over in the hospital accommodation provided by Ronald McDonald House, a charity that supports families of poorly children. We were keen to be as close to Athena as possible. It was incredibly comforting to chat to the other resident mams and dads who were in the same boat as us, and who totally understood the agony we were going through. I particularly loved the fact they just treated the pair of us like two normal parents with the same worries and concerns as everyone else. It really didn't matter to them who we were.

Tyson, bless him, was a tower of strength throughout the whole ordeal. He did his utmost to help me stay calm and positive, telling me that everything would be all right and reassuring me that our baby was receiving the best treatment in this amazing, gold-standard hospital. Tyson and I have always got through life's ups and downs by sticking together and supporting each other, and here was another case in point, even though we both agreed that nothing yet had been quite as traumatic as this. It made me realise just how robust our marriage was. We were definitely stronger together.

Our coping mechanisms differed, though. While I gained a great deal of comfort from sitting beside Athena's incubator, and being on hand to receive medical updates, Tyson found the atmosphere in ICU far too nervy and intense. He chose instead to go down the distraction therapy route, taking his mind off things by keeping himself fit with some outdoor exercise. He'd already had to postpone his departure to Las Vegas for his fight preparations, and needed to find a way to stay in shape. So he spent hours jogging around the hospital grounds and pounding the local pavements, much to the surprise of passers-by. I was totally fine with Tyson's occasional absences, knowing from past experience that his mental health was always better for having routine and discipline in his life.

As a special thank you to Alder Hey, Tyson also launched an online charity appeal while we were there, offering up one of his title belts for auction and raising over £50,000 in the process. As a family, it was the very least we could do. We'd seen for ourselves how wonderful this place was, and how brilliant the staff were, from the doctors and nurses who cared for the sick children to the volunteers who brought cups of tea to their worried parents. A host of angels, we called them.

Following consecutive days of steady progress, it looked like Athena was pulling through and plans were made to downgrade her to the high dependency unit. Finally, she was gently disconnected from the ventilator and I was allowed to cradle her in my arms. It was then my worst nightmare began. Suddenly, she became pale, floppy and unresponsive and I could see she'd stopped breathing. My blood ran cold and I let out a piercing scream. '*MY BABY'S DYING!*' I shouted, as a nurse immediately hit the red emergency buzzer. Within seconds I was surrounded by a team of doctors, who took Athena from me, laid her on the bed and began frantic resuscitation. Her heart had completely stopped. Hysterical, I rang Tyson, who was in the middle of his afternoon run. He sprinted straight back to ICU, just in time to see that the miracle-working medics had managed to revive our daughter's heartbeat and were reconnecting her to the ventilator.

From that moment onwards, Athena's condition improved dramatically. In fact, her recovery was so rapid it was barely believable. It was almost as though her heart had been reset, and was now ticking the way it should. Three days later, having passed all the necessary tests and scans with flying colours, Athena was discharged. We just had the most incredible feeling of relief when we left Alder Hey, bound for Morecambe, although our thoughts were very much with the children who remained there, along with their doting and devoted parents.

*   *   *

As I write this, Athena is approaching her second birthday, and is the happiest and healthiest little girl imaginable, with no medical issues whatsoever. Her life was saved by the Alder Hey angels that fateful day, and I'll forever be grateful for their care and expertise. But you can't go through that kind of harrowing experience without it having a huge impact on you as a person. Athena's illness made me realise just how fragile and precarious life can be – things can change in a milli-second, for better or for worse – and it doesn't matter who you are or where you come from. Sometimes life deals you a bad card, and you have to grit your teeth, hold your nerve and cope as best you can. You also need to draw on the support of your nearest and dearest and – if, like me, you're a person of faith – to trust in God.

Athena's ordeal also brought my personal priorities sharply into focus. Tyson's success in the boxing ring has given me a comfortable lifestyle that I very much appreciate – I won't lie, I adore my Chanel handbags and my Louboutin heels – but I realise they're just *things*. Over the years I've learned that it's people, not possessions, that make me happy. And it's the family that makes me happiest of all. But keeping my home and my kids in check takes a lot of time and effort, as this book illustrates. From pregnancy to parenting, and from marriage to me-time, I'll be covering the things that matter most to me. I really hope you enjoy reading about the way I lead my life and the way I face my challenges. And I hope you can find something here that helps you and your family, too.

CHAPTER ONE

LEARNING FROM MAM

MY GYPSY UPBRINGING has shaped and inspired me so much. From the way I raise my children to the way I run my home, the traditions I grew up with still influence my day-to-day life and act as my guide and compass. But while I'll always stay true to my roots, my heritage doesn't define me. More than anything, I see myself as a citizen of the world, someone who's doing her very best to be a good wife, mother, daughter, sister and friend, just like millions of other women. And while I'm very proud of my background, I'll never claim to be a spokesperson for my community. Like all sections of society, we all have our different views, values and beliefs. No individual is the same, thank goodness, and what drives one person may not drive the other.

From the days I spent living on a Traveller site in Doncaster, however, my life has taken one heck of a crazy turn. Since meeting and marrying Tyson, I've hardly stopped to take a breath. Sometimes it feels like I've been caught up in a whirlwind. In the last decade or so I've travelled the world and stayed in the best hotels. I've shopped in exclusive boutiques and dined in the finest restaurants. I've starred in a TV documentary and appeared on *Loose Women*. I've written a bestselling book and have gained over a million followers on Instagram. I can't believe how things have panned out in a relatively short space of time – I'm still only in my early thirties – but I'm truly thankful for the opportunities I've been given and the privileges I enjoy. I know for sure that Tyson feels just as blessed as I do.

But, most importantly of all, during that time Tyson and I have had the pleasure of welcoming a host of beautiful children into the world (six, as I write, with another on the way). That's our finest achievement, no question. My husband and I may enjoy the trappings of wealth – nice cars, luxury holidays, designer clothes – but, as far as we're concerned, nothing will ever match the joy of family life. Everything else pales in comparison when it comes to spending time with our loved ones.

My own parents, Lynda and Jimmy Mulroy, both hailed from Scottish Traveller stock and brought up their four kids at Tilts Farm, a large site in the middle of the South Yorkshire countryside that was home to dozens of families. I spent an idyllic childhood there, sharing a trailer with my sisters, Romain and Montana, while Mam and Dad occupied a larger one next door, and my brother Jimmy lived in an adjoining Portakabin that also housed our main kitchen, living and dining area.

The site was a real hive of activity, with plenty of things for youngsters to see and do. I have fond memories of running through the surrounding meadows at the height of summer and, on rainy days, playing with dolls and dressing-up clothes games in mine and other girls' trailers. I was related to many of these children, in some way, shape or form. The UK Traveller community is relatively small, and tends to settle in certain areas, so there are lots of links and connections.

'Tilts', as I affectionately called it, still holds a special place in my heart. I loved being part of this close-knit community and living in such a carefree environment. I also saw how the happiest families treated each other with kindness, respect and consideration, and supported one another through thick and thin. The Mulroys were a case in point.

When I was young, my dad went out to work (he owned a jewellers' business in Doncaster town centre) while Mam stayed at home to care for the children and look after the trailer, among many other responsibilities. Back then, these defined roles tended to be the norm: men were the breadwinners, while women were the

3

homemakers. Nowadays, though, things are far less rigid in our community – as with society as a whole – and more and more women are pursuing careers and going into business, especially once their children go to school.

I think it's great that my female friends and relatives are free to choose what's best for them. Some may prefer to stay at home with the kids as full-time carers, while others may decide to enter the workplace. Both are equally valid options.

I guess I'm fortunate to enjoy the best of both worlds. I've been able to raise the children myself but, thanks to support from friends and family, I've also been able to take time out now and again to pursue my business interests. Although I don't have a conventional job, I like to keep my hand in and my mind active. As well as working on my books (which I love!) I also do promotional work on social media, which often involves testing beauty products and appliances and posting up videos, often filmed at home when the kids are at school or in bed.

Since 2020 I've been making occasional appearances on ITV's *Loose Women*, too; at first this was done remotely, due to the coronavirus lockdown, but in more recent years I've had the pleasure of travelling down to the London studios to chat with my co-panellists in person, brilliant women like Coleen Nolan, Denise

Welch and Janet Street-Porter. I love going on the programme and contributing to the various debates, whether it's talking about parenting or relationships, or discussing a topic that's been dominating the news headlines.

I'm often asked if I get nervous on the *Loose Women* set, but I can't say I do. Being Tyson Fury's wife, I've become used to the presence of cameras and interviewers (especially before and after his fights) and I've learned not to let this faze me. I just try to act naturally whenever a microphone is put in front of me, and answer questions as best I can. But I'd also say that my upbringing has given me an inner confidence that helps in these situations.

'No one's above you, but no one's beneath you, either,' my mam would say to me, whenever I needed some reassurance. 'Believe in yourself, Paris.'

I remember that self-confidence when I was at college in Doncaster, and just a sixteen-year-old trainee beautician. My fellow students and I were given the simple task of politely answering a test phone call from a VIP client who wanted to make a suitable appointment. While some of the other girls crumbled about what to do and what to say, I just took it in my stride. I didn't know what all the fuss was about, to be honest. Speaking naturally and fluently was no big deal to me, no matter who was on the other end of the line. I didn't feel remotely intimidated then, and I certainly don't now.

Mam also told me to speak the truth and to be myself. She's absolutely right. I've seen public figures tying themselves in knots if they don't quite believe in what they're saying, or are pretending to be someone they're not. So if someone asks me a question, whether it's a boxing reporter or a *Loose Woman* presenter, I'll give them a straight answer, even if I know my views are not necessarily going to be shared by everyone. My attitude is 'take me as I come, like it or lump it'. Honesty is always the best policy.

I regularly get swamped with offers of work – I've been asked to appear on every TV reality show you could think of – but, nine times out of ten, I'll turn them down. Any proposal that doesn't fit into the routine of family life, or takes me away from home for too long, is politely rejected. I'll only choose things that work for me and that won't impact Tyson and the kids. They'll always be my top priority. But while I'm lucky to have achieved a good balance between my home and work life, I appreciate this isn't possible for everyone. I have the utmost respect for parents who work full time, whatever the circumstances.

* * *

It was my mam, Lynda, who taught me all my life skills, and who instilled in me the know-how and common sense that now helps me navigate family life. When I was eleven years old I made the decision to stay at home with Mam rather than continue on to high school, the plan being to attend a further education college a few years down the line. I was more than happy to follow this route – I certainly didn't need to be persuaded – and most of my friends on Tilts felt exactly the same.

Back then, Gypsy tradition dictated that this was the best way for us to learn everything about managing a household. Parents and grandparents considered it their duty and responsibility to hand down their know-how and expertise to the younger generation, especially those in their teens who needed to prepare themselves for independence. So, by choosing to stay at home instead of going to school, kids like me were given plenty of time to be taught practical skills by our elders, like how to cook a meal or change a tyre, or how to replace a broken wall tile or polish the family silver.

Our hands-on education not only helped us to safeguard the Gypsy traditions, but also taught us to be good people and decent citizens. It helped us prepare for life as parents, or partners, should that be the road we chose to go down. Our families needed reassurance that we were able to live independent lives and stand on our own two feet and, with that in mind, we were given the best grounding in how to run our own lives, whether or not we got married and had kids.

Choosing home over school in your early to mid-teens is still seen as controversial by many in the wider world – many a time I've had to argue my case for leapfrogging my secondary education on *Loose Women* – but, speaking from personal experience, I think it makes total sense. For me, pursuing this option felt like the right thing to do and I've never had any regrets.

Mam was the best guide and teacher I could have wished for. Her patience, wisdom and common sense were boundless, and she taught me all the life lessons I needed to know. She showed me how to open a bank account and how to manage a household budget. How to pay bills and how to take out insurance. How to arrange doctors' and dentists' appointments and how to apply for a passport. She spent hour upon hour sorting and filing the family's paperwork, explaining how this helped the whole household to run smoothly.

'I know it may seem boring, Paris, but one day you'll realise how important this is,' she'd say. 'If you're disorganised, your home will be disorganised.'

And then came the cleaning and tidying. Our place had to be spotless at all times, and my mother's standards were ridiculously high.

'Watch and learn, Paris,' she said each morning as she set to making our beds with careful precision, changing duvets, plumping pillows and tucking in sheets. The following day it was my turn to do the same, under Mam's watchful eye, until I performed it to perfection. After breakfast, she'd then hand me an apron and a pair of rubber gloves, before showing me how to clean the oven and hob until it shone, or how to buff the family's shoes with a cotton cloth and a tin of polish.

Mam generally stuck to a rota of jobs – filed and organised in her head, almost like clockwork – so that every household chore was performed in a regular cycle. Some were deemed daily tasks, like disinfecting sinks, mopping floors and doing the family laundry, whereas some took place weekly, like wiping down the windowsills and dusting the skirting boards. I follow a similar routine even now, whenever I give my own house a good going-over. Old habits die hard . . .

Other key jobs back then were a monthly affair, such as deep-cleaning the carpets or scrubbing the kitchen cupboards from top to bottom, before arranging their contents so everything was neat and tidy. Even now, I can't bear it when the kids mess up my cup and mug cupboard and then replace everything all higgledy-piggledy. Tyson is never guilty of that, though. In common with many people with Obsessive Compulsive

Disorder (OCD) he's fanatical about neatness, probably more so than me, and despises untidiness wherever he sees it around the house. At times his fussy and finicky behaviour can drive me crazy, but I try to turn a blind eye. It's just the way he is.

Mam treasured her family heirlooms. Ornaments, crockery and silver or crystalware were passed down through the generations or given as wedding presents, and would always be proudly displayed on sideboards or in cabinets. Keeping these precious items clean, shiny and dust-free was one of my favourite chores. I always loved buffing our antique silverware with a cloth and a bottle of Goddard's polish. I still do that job to this day, shining the beautiful sterling silver tea set that was gifted to Tyson and me when we were married.

Mam always encouraged us to keep our living space as tidy and as organised as we could, within reason. She had no problem with her kids creating clutter when we played – my bedroom floor was often strewn with Barbie dolls and Disney costumes – so long as everything was replaced in our toy box before bedtime, Mam didn't mind. It was all about thinking of others and respecting the family home.

I was taught that every household item and possession had its own place – especially in a trailer, where space was at a premium – and my mother showed me how to make good use of all our storage. So tins and cartons of food would be efficiently arranged in kitchen cupboards – carefully, not haphazardly – and in size order so they could be easily spotted and identified. Our clothes would be neatly folded in bedroom drawers, too, with equal space allocated to me, Romain and Montana.

I've tried to emulate Mam in this respect. While the atmosphere in our home can be mad and chaotic, I still try to organise myself as best as I can. Household items are always placed exactly where they should be – in the correct drawer, or the appropriate box – so I have a good idea of where everything is. If I want to lay my hands on an important travel document, or find the correct light bulb, I know exactly where to look; I simply don't have the time to scrabble around for things, or to figure out how or where to store them in the first place. If you open any drawer or cupboard in my house it will look pretty tidy and orderly. I can't bear mess or clutter.

In my teenage years I never moaned or complained when I helped my mother with the housework. Honestly, not once; no whines of 'Aw, do I have to do this, Mam?' ever passed my lips. And that's because I was more than happy to muck in. These were the jobs that Mam had allocated to me and, by acting as an extra pair of hands, I was effectively doing my bit to reduce her workload. And, not only that, by following in her footsteps – and becoming her little apprentice – I was continuing that learn-while-you-graft tradition, all the while picking up skills that would serve me well in later life. I never even grumbled when Mam tasked me with cleaning our outdoor wash block in the middle of winter.

*　　*　　*

When I was young, my mother used to say, 'Be proud of your house, Paris, whether it's a matchbox or a mansion,' and it's a message that's remained with me through to adulthood. Keeping your living area clean, tidy and presentable is a true badge of honour and Mam put so much time and effort into achieving it. Everything in our place shone and sparkled, from windows and worktops to ornaments and crockery. She couldn't relax properly if our trailer was a tip. I've definitely inherited that mind-set from her; I can't settle in the evening until the kitchen is spotless and the kids' toys are all tidied away.

And Mam was forever on stand-by mode when it came to unexpected guests. Our trailer, and later our house, was routinely clean, spruce and ready for drop-ins, and Mam was always a warm and welcoming hostess; as soon as someone set foot in the door, the kettle would be flicked on. This ever-ready approach has rubbed off on me, too, which is a good job considering the comings and goings I've experienced in my household over the years. From family and friends to members of Tyson's team, people are always stopping by or staying over. It never fazes me, even if it's unannounced. Just in case, I often cook extra meal portions (which can be frozen, if need be; nothing goes to waste!) and there are always additional seats ready to go round the Fury dinner table.

I ensure the spare room is clean and tidy, too, with fresh bedlinen, plenty of free drawer space and new toothbrushes and toothpaste beneath the sink. It's really no bother. In fact, I like having the place full of people – the more, the merrier, I say – and would much rather a chaotic household than a quiet one. I often tell Tyson we should have a revolving door installed, to cope with the constant ins and outs.

When I was about eleven, the Mulroy family moved to a three-bedroomed house in a nearby village – my parents were keen to get onto the property ladder – so there were a few more jobs to do. Each morning at nine o'clock, once Dad and Jimmy had set off for work and my sisters had gone to school, Mam would say, 'Right, Paris, let's get started, let's get moving.' After we'd both had breakfast – usually a quick piece of toast or a bowl of cereal – we'd set to our tasks. I had my area of work and Mam had hers. Mine was to ensure the upstairs landing and bedrooms were clean and tidy, while she busied herself downstairs. So I'd make all the beds, vacuum the carpets and wipe the sills and ledges, before giving the bathroom a good going-over. Meanwhile, Mam would whizz around the kitchen, lounge and dining room with her array of cloths, sprays and brushes. We had both floors all done and dusted (quite literally) in an hour, after which we might tackle a couple of extra chores in the kitchen, maybe cleaning the oven or disinfecting the fridge.

That would often leave the afternoons free for us to have some quality mother-and-daughter time together. Occasionally we'd go shopping, either on Doncaster high street or in Sheffield's Meadowhall centre, and sometimes we'd meet up for lunch with one of Mam's friends, whose children I'd happily play with. We'd also visit the local leisure centre, where we'd either have a swim or attend the gym (I loved relaxing in the sauna or steam room afterwards). On Wednesdays and Fridays, Mam would drive me to a nearby community centre for my regular learning and education sessions, laid on for Traveller kids by Doncaster Council.

Getting home about three o'clock, before Romain and Montana returned from school, Mam would start to prepare the evening family meal. She preferred to get on with it herself – too many cooks spoil the broth, as they say – but I'd often take time to observe what she was doing. She'd carefully plan the meals for the week

– good, old-fashioned meat-and-two-veg staples – and would make a list of all the individual recipe items, so she only bought what was needed. This allowed her to stay within her budget (my family were always careful not to overspend) as well as ensuring minimal food waste.

Mam gave me a lot of advice about how to economise with my food shopping. At the supermarket, she'd teach me to check for the longest sell-by dates, and show me how to save money by buying in bulk or choosing buy-one-get-one-free deals. She also told me that, if you spent your cash carefully, you could then afford some special weekly treats like a leg of lamb or a fillet steak from our local butcher.

My mother cooked from scratch most nights, making us filling and wholesome dishes that the whole family enjoyed. More often than not she stuck to a rota of nutritious meals that saw us eating ham, cabbage and mash one night, perhaps, then steak Diane and chips the next, and stove tatties (an oven-baked dish of sausages, potatoes and onions) after that. Any leftovers would be frozen for another day.

If Mam had time to do a pudding, she might bake something traditional like apple pie and custard or chocolate sponge and ice cream. She dished up some American cuisine, too, having spent much of her childhood travelling around the United States, and would knock up lovely fluffy pancakes, served with sliced fruit, or – if we were really lucky – she'd bake some banana cream pies. They were *so* delicious. I keep meaning to ask her to make some for my kids one day. I'm sure Granny's puddings would go down a treat.

Each Sunday, like most British families, the Mulroys got around the dining table to enjoy a roast dinner. We'd often go out to eat, too, heading over to a local pub that laid on a decent carvery. The Sunday roast is a tradition I've continued myself with the Furys, despite the vast amount of time it takes to prepare (especially for my huge brood!). It's a total winner in our household; a couple of my kids are fussy eaters but even they're guaranteed to wolf down a roast dinner, especially if I've bought a joint of beef or a leg of lamb from our fantastic local butcher.

'No better meal in the world . . .' Tyson will often say as he drowns his plate in Bisto gravy.

* * *

To keep the Mulroy household running smoothly, each family member played their part. We all mucked in; my dad and Jimmy tackled most of the outdoor tasks, for example, like sweeping the yard, cutting back trees or sorting out the car maintenance. Montana did her bit, too – many hands make light work, as they say – although my elder sister Romain wasn't always able to help out. Hers is quite a tragic story. When she was a baby she contracted a particularly severe case of whooping cough, which affected her brain and led to permanent learning disabilities. Romain went to a local special school for years; this was another reason we didn't move around much as a family, because it was important she had stability and continuity. Nowadays, my big sister lives a very happy and active life but, as she has the mental age of a five-year-old, she'll never be fully independent. She is still looked after by my parents, who care for her with such kindness and compassion, and without any fuss or drama.

In fact, over the years Mam and Dad have taught me a lot about coping with life's challenges. They've helped me realise that when things don't always go to plan – like Romain's situation – you have to dig deep, stay calm and get on with things as best you can. Whenever I've experienced my own family setbacks I've always tried to channel my parents' level-headedness.

Some people assume I've always led a charmed life, but they'd be mistaken. I've faced plenty of tough times, whether it's been coping with Tyson's period of depression or dealing with medical emergencies, and there have been moments when I've felt my emotions wobble and my defences crumble. However, by invoking the strength and resilience of my parents, I've dragged myself through those rough patches and have been able to pick myself up, dust myself down and put my best foot forward. As a mother with children who rely on me, there's no possibility of just stopping and quitting. I just have to keep things together for their sake. My mam was exactly the same, and would often refer to herself as the 'glue' of the family. Like her, I see it as my duty to keep my husband and kids on an even keel.

Raising children is a source of huge pride to my family – to us, they're a gift from God – and it probably explains why I've chosen to have so many. I just love the whole process of expecting a baby, welcoming them into the family and nurturing them through life. I guess I'm following in the footsteps of my maternal grandmother, who brought up four sons and four daughters, all of whom were born within a ten-year time span. Lynda, my mam, was the eldest of her brood and acted as a second mother to the other siblings. And that experience, in tandem with raising her own four children, shaped her into the best parent and grandparent you could ever hope for.

There's simply nothing my mam doesn't know about childcare. Over the years she's accumulated a wealth of knowledge, from curbing toddler tantrums to changing babies' nappies. I remember once going to a baby shower where one of the party games was putting a nappy on a doll, blindfolded, with the winner being the person who did it in the quickest time. Mam smashed every single round; she could literally do it with her eyes shut.

I've learned so much from her, in many different ways, and if I prove to be half the mother she is I'll be delighted. Don't get me wrong, my father was also a great role model – you couldn't fault his work ethic, and his sense of family duty – but he'll be the first to admit that Mam was the parenting expert.

First and foremost, my mother was always unfailingly kind, patient and caring, especially so with Romain, who naturally demanded more of her attention. In terms of discipline, she was firm but fair; she wouldn't tolerate bad manners or disrespectful behaviour, and would encourage us to treat other people as we wished to be treated ourselves. Along with her serious side, Mam had a fun-loving nature and a great sense of humour that meant there were always lots of laughs and smiles in our household. She loved hosting parties for special occasions, because that meant getting all her friends and family together in the same room for a good time. Her glass-half-full approach to life was fantastic – it still is – and it's an attitude I try to channel myself.

* * *

Home is so much more than bricks and mortar and, house-proud though I am, of much more importance to me are the people inside it. I totally agree with the person who said that 'home is where the heart is,' because nothing makes me more content than hearing the children playing and laughing upstairs with their cousins, for instance, or having a brew and a biscuit with my mam and sisters around the kitchen table. My home in Morecambe has become the perfect family hub – I try my best to make it warm and welcoming – and I adore being surrounded by my Fury and Mulroy relatives. They're the people who know me best, and in whose company I can completely relax. It's so important that I can talk to them about anything, and trust them with anything.

In this respect I've taken a leaf out of Mam's book; she always taught me to keep my loved ones close and to maintain strong family ties. Preserving those bonds was incredibly important to her – 'blood's thicker than water,' she'd say – even if some members of our extended family lived further away. While Tilts Farm was very family-orientated when we stayed there – it was common for three or four generations to live side by side – most of my extended family lived elsewhere in the UK. My beloved Granny Mary moved around the south of England (and spent time in America, too) and my dad's family were based up in the north-east, near Newcastle upon Tyne. Despite the distance, we'd visit them often. Occasionally the entire clan would congregate at St Boswells Fair, a Travellers' gathering in the Scottish Borders, and I'd love roaming around the fair with all my friends and cousins.

Coming from a close-knit family, I do my utmost to stay in touch with my loved ones nowadays. I think it's really important for my sons and daughters to get to know their cousins, aunts and uncles, and for the grown-ups to see the youngsters flourishing. Not only do I want my kids to make lots of happy childhood memories, just like I did, I also want them to know where they come from, and who all their relatives are. My parents and siblings visit regularly – there have been plenty of Fury birthday parties and christenings for them to attend, let's be honest! – and I often return the compliment by travelling over to them, too. I'm particularly close to my Aunt Romain, my mam's youngest sister.

Granny Mary is in her mid-nineties now and, while physically frail, is still a force of nature. I've always looked up to her – she's one of the most stylish and glamorous women I know – and she's had a huge influence on my life. Like my mam, she's a very strong, proud and upstanding woman. She's always taught me to put my best foot forward, whether that means maintaining a positive attitude at all times – especially when the going gets tough – or keeping yourself looking smart and presentable, even if you're just nipping out to the shops.

'Dress tidily, brush your hair, and put a little bit of make-up on,' she'll say. 'Always make an effort, Paris. Don't just roll out of bed.'

I also try to catch up with my extended family as much as I can, face to face wherever possible – I have dozens of cousins, nieces and nephews – but I also chat on the phone and swap messages and photos via texts or WhatsApp. Sometimes it's hard to imagine how we communicated before the introduction of mobiles and social media. I'm probably not the only person to feel a little uncomfortable with modern technology – I'm quite wary of computers and websites, so much so that I rarely shop online – and sometimes I still wish we wrote postcards and spoke on landlines!

And, while we might not see each other for a couple of months at a time, my relatives and I are close enough to maintain those strong connections. Whenever we get together, it's very much a case of picking up where we left off. I'm the same with my in-laws, too. I love catching up with Tyson's brothers and their wives, and always encourage him to keep connected with his side of the family, most of whom live over in Cheshire. Picking up the phone does slip his mind, especially if he's shut away in fight camp, and he'll occasionally need a nudge in the right direction. Promising to keep in touch is often easier than actually doing it.

'Have you called your brothers, Tyson?' I'll say. 'And have you checked in with your mam and your dad? Don't forget, family comes first.'

We both take great pride in our families, and will drop everything if there's a friend or relative in need. Growing up at Tilts Farm, I saw community spirit in action all the time. If one of the mothers on the site fell ill, and was unable to look after her children, another woman would offer to care for the little ones. If one of the fathers' cars broke down, and they couldn't get to work, another dad would be on hand to give them a lift, and then repair the engine. Everybody would band together to help each other.

On a wider scale, lots of charitable work was undertaken, too, with members of our community frequently raising money to help local families or organisations who might be struggling. I like to think that spirit of goodwill lives on with me and Tyson. The vast majority of Gypsies and Travellers are kind-hearted and well-intentioned people, contrary to what others may say.

23

So, as we go about our day-to-day business, Tyson and I will always uphold those family values and embrace that sense of togetherness. We'll forever remind our children to be proud of the people we are, and the traditions we treasure. Passing down that legacy is so important to us, and as my mam often says to me, 'Don't ever forget where you come from, Paris . . .'

Chapter Two

A STRANGE AND CRAZY EXPERIENCE

As the mother of six children – an old hand, you might say – I think I've learned a fair bit about having babies. I had my first child when I was nineteen – my daughter Venezuela – and, in 2013, my eldest son Prince came along. A few years later I had three babies in quick succession – Tyson, Valencia and Adonis all arrived in the space of two and a half years – and, in 2021, I gave birth to little Athena. I'm expecting baby number seven right now, and who knows if there'll be any more . . .

Having a baby is incredible, in every sense of the word. The whole process, from beginning to end, still fills me with wonder. The way your baby grows. The way your body adapts. The way your mood swings from excitement one minute, to nervousness the next. I remember Tyson once saying that this journey was 'a strange and crazy experience'. He was speaking from a partner's perspective, of course, but he wasn't wrong. It can feel so natural and normal in some respects, yet so weird and wacky in others. But having a baby never fails to amaze and delight me.

I often compare carrying a child with one of Tyson's title fight victories. First, you make the big announcement, which gets everybody really excited. Then you have months of preparation – the long build-up – in which you have to look after your body and listen to lots of advice. As the weeks go by, and your big moment looms, your nerves begin to jangle, as you wonder what's in store for you, and how you're going to cope. When the day finally arrives, it can be traumatic or triumphant – or a mixture of both – and when it's all over and done with you're full of joy, relief and pride. And a few months later, when everything's calmed down, you start to consider doing it all over again.

I always knew I wanted to have children . . . and plenty of them. I loved hearing Mam's tales about her seven siblings – they seemed to have a whale of a time, growing up in America – and I really liked the idea of raising my own big brood, once I'd found the right person to settle down with. I had plenty of childcare practice on Tilts Farm – the site was swarming with kids – and I'd always offer my services if any of them needed minding or entertaining. I liked taking the little ones to the park or playing daft board games, and got such a buzz from keeping them safe and making them laugh. There's no nicer sound than a toddler with a fit of the giggles.

Luckily, Tyson shared my long-held desire to have children. We fell madly in love as teenagers and within weeks we were excitedly talking about getting married and having babies. I think I told him I wanted ten. Like me, he hailed from a large family, and – other than some serious boxing ambitions – he wanted nothing more out of life than to raise a family of mini-Furys.

Not that we planned to have our first baby so quickly, though. We'd only been married a few months when I discovered I was expecting (I found out in an Asda toilet cubicle, of all places). I'd been behaving a little strangely for a couple of days, and, when I randomly bit a chunk from a block of Cheddar in the supermarket, Tyson decided this was a food craving. He immediately came to the conclusion that I was expecting and reckoned I should do a test, there and then. I couldn't believe my eyes when I saw the blue line gradually appear. I felt shocked, but thrilled.

'Don't you *dare* tell my mam yet,' I said to Tyson as we drove home. I was convinced she'd be furious. I was only nineteen, which was still fairly young to be having a child, and no doubt she'd worry I was rushing into things. My concerns were unfounded, though; Mam was over-joyed when we finally plucked up the courage to tell her.

'Don't be stupid, Paris, as *if* I'd ever be cross with you,' she said. 'Having a baby is always good news.'

Other than confiding in close family, we kept our news to ourselves until the twelve-week ultrasound scan. Like many parents-to-be, we wanted to have that assurance that everything was OK with the baby. Those early stages can be a risky time, of course, and neither Tyson nor I wanted to tempt fate.

As we've gone on to have more children, however, our secrecy pact has fallen by the wayside, largely due to Tyson. I've never known a man get so excited about his wife falling pregnant, so much so that he'll often reveal the news to my friends and family before I do, despite my request to hang fire for a few weeks. Worse still, my darling husband has been known to blurt out our baby news on live television, which he did when I was expecting Little Tyson, Valencia *and* Adonis. He just can't help himself. He's got to broadcast it to the world. The following day the newspapers will run a 'Fury's Baby Joy' story, and my phone will ring off its hinges.

'Yep, he's gone and blabbed again,' I'll sigh when the umpteenth friend calls to congratulate me. 'He can't hold his own pee, that man . . .'

* * *

I realise that having babies and raising children isn't for everyone, though. There are some women who don't want to have kids, who perhaps don't possess that maternal instinct, and I totally respect that. People have other plans in life, and pursue different paths, and that doesn't always include being a parent. I'll never judge anyone for the choices they make; you should do what's best for you, and not feel pressured otherwise. There are also women who do not have that option, and who are unable to have children. Speaking as someone who has suffered baby loss, I know how devastating this can be. So, while I'm here to tell my story and share my experiences, I do appreciate that my words may not chime with everybody.

It's fair to say that pregnancy suits me pretty well. Other than a medical condition that affects me in the later stages, I'm lucky in that I feel quite healthy through-out and am pretty much able to stick to my normal daily routine. As someone who has a family to raise and a household to run, I try not to let my bump hold me back. People who know me will tell you I'm a no-fuss, no-frills, keep-calm-and-carry-on type of person. 'She just rolled with it . . .' will probably be etched on my tombstone.

Managing my day-to-day life is a little more difficult when Tyson's away, though, which is often the case when a fight is looming. There have been a couple of occasions when he's been holed up in a US training camp for a few months while I've been at home in Morecambe, heavily pregnant, holding the fort. I miss him a lot – especially his emotional and practical support – but it's in my nature to cope, not mope. There are plenty of amazing single parents out there who manage perfectly well – on a permanent basis, too – so there's no reason why I can't do the same.

My nine-month journey is a little different for each pregnancy, of course – no experience is ever the same – and some progress more smoothly than others. But when it comes down to it, I love expecting a baby – it releases lots of my happy hormones – and the whole process suits me well (I'm often told that I have that special glow). I've also found that the more babies I've had, the more I've learned along the way, which means I'm less likely to worry about check-ups, tests and twinges. Nowadays, I tend to know what to expect; I can better recognise signs and symptoms and won't hesitate to ask for help and advice if necessary.

During the first trimester (up until week 12) I occasionally suffer with morning sickness, but not severely so. If I ever feel a bit queasy, sipping a glass of water and nibbling on a piece of dry toast can help a little. My granny's remedy of eating ginger biscuits – (the spice prevents nausea, apparently) doesn't work for me. And, like many expectant mothers, in those early months I completely go off certain foodstuffs. I hate the taste of tea and coffee, for instance, and can't stomach any rich, oily foods. I remember being in Florida when I was first expecting with Valencia, and gagging at the mere sight of the hotel's huge breakfast fry-ups. I'd always opt for fruit salad or cereal instead.

When I'm pregnant I do my best to follow the food and drink guidelines, although they've chopped and changed a bit between Baby One and Baby Six. So I generally avoid seafood and shellfish, as well as meat pâtés and soft, unpasteurised cheeses. I try to eat lots of healthy and wholesome food, so plenty of fruit and vegetables as well as lean meat and dairy products. And, while I make an effort to moderate my intake of sweet treats, I have been known to send Tyson out to the shops to grab me a chocolate bar and a fizzy drink. Like many partners of hormonal pregnant women, he does his utmost to stay on my good side, bless him. He's learned not to cross an expectant mother with raging hormones!

I don't generally have many cravings, but in the past I have gravitated towards beige-coloured food, from bread and biscuits to cakes and crackers (that's quite common, I'm told). As regards vitamins and supplements, at breakfast I'll take a multivitamin tablet that contains folic acid, as recommended by my midwife. She'll also recommend that I stay away from alcohol, which I do as a rule, save perhaps a piña colada while I'm on holiday or a rosé spritzer on Christmas Day. I'm not a big drinker anyway – I can take it or leave it – so it's no massive hardship; I'll just substitute it with a glass of chilled water or orange cordial.

In common with many expectant mothers, my energy levels take a dive during those early weeks, and I'll often become quite tired, particularly at the end of the day. Luckily, I sleep pretty well at night, and I don't need much sleep to function. It gets a little more uncomfortable as time goes by, and you're a little more restless because it's hard to settle, especially if the baby's kicking. And because your body shape has changed so much, you often have to adopt a totally different sleeping position, perhaps resting on your right side instead of your left. I've never bothered with one of those long pillows to go between my knees, though; I've just used a couple of normal ones. The last month of pregnancy is definitely more of a challenge when it comes to sleep. I remember once tossing and turning in the middle of the night and almost getting stuck, like a beached whale, and having to ask Tyson to gently roll me over because I couldn't do it myself.

During the day I try to relax and take it easy, allowing myself plenty of rest when it's needed. Over the years

I've learned how to listen to my body, and to know when it's time to slow down. As I've had more children, it's not surprising that fitting in some R&R has become increasingly difficult. It can be hard to wind down with three noisy youngsters running riot. There's only two and a half years between Little Tyson, Valencia and Adonis, so controlling them became a bit of a struggle when I was carrying Athena. When it all got too much I'd lure the three of them into one bedroom, somewhere nice and safe for them to watch some kids' DVDs while I had a lie-down (although I always kept an eye on them).

I try not to get too hung up about the housework if I'm feeling particularly weary. Don't get me wrong, I love nothing more than a clean, tidy and organised house, but there are times when I've assessed a huge pile of washing or a bedroom littered with toys, shrugged my shoulders and thought, *Oh, it'll be there tomorrow.* It's one of my favourite sayings, as my friends will testify. Jobs and chores always get done eventually . . .

I don't always get this balance right, however. During my earlier pregnancies I regularly overdid it, trying to be all things to all people and running around like a headless chicken. I often refused help from family and friends, particularly when Tyson was away, simply because I didn't want to be a burden to anyone. I've wised up with my more recent pregnancies. For my health's sake, I've learned to swallow my pride and accept these kind offers of assistance. Every little helps, as they say, whether it's my mam cooking our family meal or my friend picking up the kids from school.

In slight contrast to the first trimester, I usually sail through the second pregnancy phase with very few issues. It's then when my baby bump starts to show, too. When I was expecting Venezuela, I was really conscious of putting on weight. It was my very first baby – everything felt so new and unknown – and I'd convinced myself I was going to blow up like a balloon. I've always been quite slim but for some reason I had it in my mind I was going to become enormous, waddling around the place and getting stuck in car doors.

As things turned out, I only gained two stone – I was 'all bump', as they say – and, two days after the birth, was able to fit back into my pre-pregnancy clothes. No doubt being nineteen years old had a bearing, as you tend to ping back into shape much quicker when you're younger. But I'm lucky in that all my baby bumps have been quite neat and compact, so I've never needed to shift many extra pounds afterwards (although I did join a gym after my sixth child Athena was born). With my more recent pregnancies, and with an older head on my shoulders, I've been far less bothered about my shape and size while I'm carrying, which isn't a bad thing. As far as I'm concerned, there are far more important issues to concern myself with, like giving birth to a healthy child. I accept myself for who I am these days, whether or not I can fit into my old clothes.

I don't tend to do much organised exercise when I'm expecting a baby. So no special gym sessions or aqua-swim classes for me, but I do appreciate that other women find them really useful and therapeutic. To keep myself fit, I try to do a lot of walking. I don't do anything too strenuous – no hiking up hills or scrambling up cliffs – but will happily go for a gentle stroll along the Morecambe promenade with Tyson and the kids, perhaps stopping off for an ice lolly or a bag of chips, the usual seaside fare. But if I'm heavily pregnant in winter I hardly go out at all – I just hibernate, like a big hedgehog!

It's usually midway through the pregnancy that, all being well, I feel the baby kicking for the first time. It felt so bizarre when it happened for the first time with my first child Venezuela. It felt alien, in fact. *What the heck is going on here?* I remember thinking to myself. It totally freaked me out that there was a miniature human moving around inside me, making her presence felt with a swift dig of a heel or a poke of an elbow. Eventually I'd become accustomed to her night-time kicks, although I can't say it ever filled me with an earth mother-like sense of joy. I still find it a bit strange and weird, if I'm being totally honest.

And as for maternity wear . . . I don't usually bother! I continue wearing my normal day-to-day clothes until they start to feel a little snug, usually as I near the seven-month stage, and then I'll invest in a few items in a larger size rather than head to the maternity section. I much prefer to wear baggy linen trousers or stretchy jogging bottoms than those jeans with elastic panels at the front; I just find them really uncomfortable. Even if I'm attending a glamorous party with Tyson, I'll just wear a Lycra or maxidress a couple of sizes larger, most likely bought from a high street store like River Island or TK Maxx. There's no point spending silly money on something I might wear once or twice. I know that maternity wear is a lot more varied and stylish than it used to be, but I just don't feel the need to add it to my wardrobe.

*   *   *

I never demand to be spoiled and pampered during pregnancy – it's just not my thing – so Tyson is under no obligation to run me bubble baths or give me foot massages. The biggest indulgence I have is treating myself to some decent skincare products to keep me nice and moisturised as the weeks pass by. Following a recommendation from Mam, I've become a huge fan of a well-known body oil (clue: it comes in a plain-looking orange and white box) and have slathered it on during all my pregnancies. I swear by the stuff. After carrying six kids I haven't got any stretch marks – not a single one – and although my skin is pretty supple anyway I'm convinced this magic oil has got something to do with it. So that's my top tip for any mothers-to-be out there!

The majority of the final trimester – the last leg – is usually quite straightforward for me, give or take the occasional bout of backache. It's around this time that I'll start to feel more tired, of course, not only because I'm carrying a big bump around, but also because it becomes physically harder to manage the other children, particularly the younger ones. I can't lift them up or chase after them as I'd normally do, so Tyson or the older kids will often have to intervene.

Things can change a little when I hit the thirty-week mark, though. After that point I have to be monitored closely because when I'm pregnant I'm prone to a liver condition called cholestasis. Although it doesn't leave me feeling ill in any way, it has potential complications for the baby, which means I'm often in and out of hospital. I only realised I was a sufferer when I was pregnant with Venezuela – she had to be induced at thirty-eight weeks as a result – and it was similar with all the other five, too. It came as a big shock when I was first diagnosed, but with subsequent pregnancies I've come to expect it and can plan accordingly. The midwives and doctors are forewarned and forearmed and keep a really close eye on me, giving me plenty of check-ups and blood tests.

Maintaining a good relationship with your midwife and other clinicians during your pregnancy is essential, I think. Tyson and I are huge supporters of our National Health Service and I'm proud to say that all my children have been born in NHS hospitals. The care I've received there has been excellent, so I've never seen any reason to go privately. I've been lucky to have the same community midwife for my last four babies, too, which means I've been able to build a great connection over the years. I ask her questions all the time – if I'm ever unsure or unhappy about something, I'll speak up – and I always ensure I'm aware of my rights as a mother-to-be and as a new mother, as well as the care and services I'm entitled to. There's plenty of advice about pregnancy on the NHS website too, but because I'm not the best web user (I get lost in all the links and pages) I much prefer to get my information face to face, straight from the horse's mouth. I've always got my mam to ask, too. She's a mine of information.

I never miss any pregnancy clinics or midwife checks; you really can't be too careful. There have been times in the past, however, when I've walked into the health centre and been met with a few surprised expressions when I'm recognised, waiting my turn in an NHS clinic like everyone else. People might automatically assume I'd use private healthcare, unaware that I'm the NHS's biggest fan. But away from all the craziness and excitement of the boxing ring, Tyson and I try to live very normal lives, and I'm just another mother who has the same worries and concerns as everyone else.

The only time I've ever had any kind of preferential treatment has been with my two most recent pregnancies. With the older four children, I wasn't nearly as recognisable as I am now, so I could attend clinics quite anonymously without fear of anyone tipping off the press that I was having a baby. By the time I was expecting Adonis and Athena, however (and thanks in large part to a fly-on-the-wall documentary we did for ITV in 2020), I'd become more of a public figure. So it was my midwife who suggested home visits during those very early days, to protect my privacy and minimise any stress, particularly as I had a history of baby loss. Once my pregnancy was made public (invariably by Tyson . . . grrrr!) I returned to clinic-based checks as normal.

I only want to say a few words about baby loss here.

Those of you who read my memoir, *Love & Fury*, will know about the trauma I experienced when I suffered both a stillbirth and a miscarriage. Opening up in my memoir was the right thing to do – I wanted to speak honestly and candidly, in order to help other women – but I found the process of reliving it incredibly difficult, and I never hide the fact that I feel very uncomfortable discussing that time in my life. If anyone mentions baby loss to me I tend to clam up and change the subject, not because I'm feeling any less grief and heartache than anyone else, but because I prefer not to dwell on my loss and dredge up those memories. What happened was awful – for me and for Tyson – but I've since allowed myself to move forward, slowly but surely.

I was extremely touched by the reception I got from readers of my first book, not just on social media but from people in the street. I think my experience struck a chord with many women who've gone through similar trauma themselves – it made them realise they weren't alone; and that gave me so much comfort too. Tackling this issue, and hearing other women's stories (some of which are incredibly tragic), also makes me realise how fortunate I am to have been able to give birth to more children. It's a blessing I shall never, ever take for granted.

* * *

While we're always careful to prepare our older children for the arrival of a new baby, Tyson and I are a little old-fashioned when it comes to breaking the news. When I was expecting Adonis, and then Athena, we told the other kids we'd arranged for the special delivery of a new baby, which the stork would be dropping off in a few months' time. I know it sounds a bit daft, but it's our way of preserving their innocence (while it lasts) and preventing awkward questions, which we might not feel comfortable answering. The eldest two, Venezuela and Prince, will raise their eyebrows when we tell them this – they're a bit more savvy these days – but the little ones are easily convinced.

'She's eaten too many cakes, kids,' Tyson will say whenever they've asked why Mam's belly is growing bigger by the day.

I've only had one gender reveal, and I can say, hand on heart, that I'll never do it again. Despite my best intentions it was a total and utter flop. Beforehand I'd convinced myself that it would be such fun – and gender reveals were all the rage on Instagram – so when I was expecting Athena I bought my own confetti cannon to let off in the house one afternoon. Tyson wasn't remotely impressed by the idea. He didn't care if we were having a boy or a girl, and thought it was all a bit silly and unnecessary. I should have listened to him, because when the cannon blasted out its girly pink contents, three of the kids stormed off because they wanted a brother. And then I realised as well that it contained fluorescent powder, which badly stained the white grout of my very expensive floor tiles. I spent days scrubbing them white again, cursing myself that I'd not performed our gender reveal outside, like any sensible person.

Tyson and I have always found out the sex of our baby during the second routine ultrasound scan. For me, it's an easy decision. I've never been a big fan of surprises – I prefer to be in control – and I'm far too curious and inquisitive to be kept in suspense for so long. Being a practical person, I also like to plan ahead, whether that's choosing a name or buying baby clothes. And neither Tyson nor I are ever really bothered if we have a boy or a girl. We're fine either way and are more concerned that our baby is born healthy. The fact we've ended up with three of each has been a happy coincidence.

As regards baby showers, I've only ever had one, prior to Venezuela's birth. Back then, the trend had yet to take off properly in the UK. However, my mam's time in America meant she knew all about these girly get-togethers. She also loves a party, and was keen to host one for my first baby. She invited about thirty close friends and family members for a brilliant evening of food, drink and conversation (much of it baby-related) and I was extremely grateful to receive an array of fabulous gifts – including clothes and equipment for Venezuela, and pamper packs for me – which was much appreciated since I was effectively starting from scratch.

While I enjoyed it, I didn't feel the need to repeat it with my other pregnancies. With Prince, my second-born, I was in and out of hospital towards the end of my term (cholestasis had reared its head again) and wasn't in the mood for a big social event. I felt similar when I had Little Tyson, four years later. When I was expecting my fourth, Valencia, my younger sister happened to be pregnant at the same time with her first baby, and Mam was keen for a double celebration.

'Why don't I throw a joint baby shower?' she asked.

'No, let Montana enjoy her own,' I replied.

I didn't want to take any of the limelight away from her – having your first child is extra-special and so I was happy to stand aside. It was a case of 'been there, done that' and by that point I'd accumulated plenty of baby gear and gadgets and would have felt guilty accepting presents I no longer really needed. That's not to say I wasn't just as thrilled to be expecting my fourth baby as my first.

By their very nature, baby showers can give you a great opportunity to learn about other women's experiences with pregnancy and childcare, as there's always lots of baby chat and much discussion of issues like feeding and sleeping. My friends and family are always a fabulous source of information. At any one time, there's usually someone who's expecting – or has expected – and who's happy to give out advice. Obviously, the more children I've had, the more knowledge I've amassed myself, but there are still occasions where I need a sounding board or a second opinion. But I've never felt compelled to pick up a baby manual or a childcare book. I've had all the advice I've ever needed from NHS professionals or my own family network or friendship group.

That being said, now that I've carried six children I've become one of those wise women myself! When Molly-Mae (she's the partner of Tyson's brother Tommy) was expecting her baby, Bambi, we had a few chats, which was nice, although I doubt she'll need too much childcare advice from me. She's an incredibly smart, sensible and switched-on young woman, and is showing all the signs of being a brilliant mother. And, like Tyson, Tommy is a fantastic father too.

Expectant mothers are often advised to get their hospital bag ready in good time. I'm used to packing mine around the thirty-week mark, since I tend to get called into hospital earlier than most. Clothes-wise, it usually contains two cheap nightgowns (that I can throw away

44

afterwards, if need be), two decent pairs of pyjamas, a dressing gown and a pair of slippers. I'll also chuck in the usual toiletries, cosmetics and accessories: a hairbrush, a toothbrush, my wash kit, a small make-up bag (including essential lip balm!) and my favourite body oil. In the other compartment I'll pack the baby gear, which usually comprises disposable nappies, a changing mat and a few formula milk bottles (the little ready-to-feed ones you can use straight away). A stack of plain babygrows are a must – enough for frequent changes – but I'll always add a nice outfit, perhaps for that all-important first photograph. And I don't know how common this is, but I always take a nice cot bedding set, too, because I don't like seeing my baby in that bare plastic bed!

Some mothers-to-be find themselves entering 'nesting' mode a few weeks before their due date, when they feel a sudden urge to tidy the house from top to bottom in preparation for the new baby. That doesn't really happen to me, though, because – without sounding too saintly – my house is pretty shipshape to begin with. I'm forever vacuuming carpets and reorganising cupboards anyway, whether I'm expecting or not, so you could say I was in a permanent state of nesting.

When it gets closer to the Big Day I do start to get a little bit twitchy, and will find myself ticking off a mental checklist: is the bottle steriliser working OK? Have I got enough blankets for the Moses basket? Are the toys and teddies all nice and clean? I'll get all the baby clothes ready, making sure I've got enough of the essential indoor and outdoor items and sorting them into age order (newborn, 0–3 months, 3–6 months and so on). I've accumulated lots of babywear over the years, and am quite happy to recycle garments that are still in good condition, whether it's using them for my own children, giving them to someone I know or taking them to the charity shop. Only the really stained or scruffy items will go in the bin.

Some outfits are particularly sentimental to me – a dress worn on a first birthday, or a cute Santa's elf costume – so I'll carefully wash and iron them before packing them away, with a view to using them again. These special garments have become family heirlooms, passed down from child to child. Athena still wears beautiful smock dresses that were bought for Venezuela a decade previously, and looks just as pretty as her older sister!

We also have a really sweet family tradition whereby a little gold ring with a tiny diamond is passed down for the baby daughters to wear. My mam initially bought this item of jewellery for Romain, before handing it on to me and Montana, who have in turn passed it down to our own girls. I think it's a lovely thing to do.

As for newborn baby equipment, I invest in good basics: a decent pram, a sturdy car seat, a safe and secure cot and a comfy Moses basket. I don't always have to buy new, of course, because good-quality products can last me a few years and may span two or three babies. Also, Traveller tradition dictates that your parents will offer to buy the larger items, like cots and prams, which has certainly been the case with our family, and which I'm very grateful for. The way things are going, Tyson and I might have to shell out for lots of prams in the future as our new grandchildren arrive on the scene!

When it comes to these items, I go for function over looks every single time. I don't follow trends or fashions; to me, durability and practicality take precedence. I like my pram to have nice big wheels, for example, because it just feels more stable and less wobbly when I'm pushing it. When I was expecting Adonis, I remember my mam telling me to choose the safest, strongest-looking cot I could find, nothing too fragile or flimsy. Something that the two toddlers, Tyson and Valencia, wouldn't be able to climb up and tip over, with awful consequences. Another great piece of advice from Mam.

* * *

47

I've always found it really useful to write a birth plan. Many midwives will encourage you to do so because it allows the healthcare team to get a good idea of your preferences when you're in the delivery room. So I'll jot down a list of all my hopes and requirements for the labour and the birth, ranging from which pain relief I favour to whether I want the baby to be handed to me straight away. A birth plan is a very personal thing, of course – and will differ from woman to woman – so I'm not going to lecture anyone here about my own likes and dislikes. What I would say, though, is that I usually try to remain open-minded; after six births, I can definitely say that things don't always go as expected, and there have been occasions when I've had to adjust my priorities for the benefit of me and the baby.

I'm a big fan of birthing partners, too, if you're lucky enough to have someone who can take that role (I appreciate that's not always the case). For the most part I've had Mam and Tyson with me, other than my first birth – which Tyson missed as he was boxing in Ireland – and my most recent birth, which Mam missed due to Covid-19 regulations. We had a total trauma after Athena's delivery, with her serious heart issues, and part of me wonders whether Mam's absence had a bearing. I'm a little bit superstitious and, the one time she wasn't there, everything turned nightmarish. Put it this way, when I have my next baby my mother will be in that labour suite, even if it means smuggling her through a window.

For me, having a birthing partner is all about having moral support and an extra pair of eyes. When you're in the throes of labour, it's good to have someone to hold your hand and dab your brow (or someone to occasionally yell at, as Tyson will testify). A birthing partner can also, in certain situations, stand back and assess things on your behalf. They can act as your voice, your advocate. You may not be in a fit state to make a judgement, but that person might spot something that doesn't look right or that needs to be queried. Nobody knows me better than Mam and Tyson, and it means the world to have their help and support when I need it most.

As for pain relief during labour, as a rule I'll accept whatever's on offer if it's going to ease that wave of contractions. When I was expecting Venezuela, my first baby, I'll never forget what my Aunt Tawny said (she's one of Mam's sisters, a proper character who's not known for holding back her opinion). One day I told her I was going to try for a natural birth, the plan being to shun any medication and rely on my inner strength and willpower.

'Are you *f*****g* crazy, Paris?' she laughed. 'Would you go and get a tooth pulled out and not have your jaw numbed?'

49

Aunt Tawny's words struck a chord, and I soon changed my mind. With all my babies, I've accepted all manner of drugs and jabs when my contractions have gone into overdrive. So I've consented to gas and air, or a spinal epidural, and will gladly do so again if need be. I've spoken to women who've been made to feel guilty for receiving pain relief, which is plainly ridiculous. They should do what's right for them, whether that's accepting or declining medication. I'll always take what I'm offered, and will never be made to feel bad about it.

Having an epidural during Venezuela's birth was quite an eventful experience, as it happened, but more for the midwife than me. Just as the jab was being administered into my back, the anaesthetist somehow tipped over the tall metal pole that connected the drip, which hit the midwife's head and knocked her out. Now, I've been used to seeing boxers hitting the deck (usually Tyson's opponents), but not a nurse. It was like something out of a *Carry On* film. Everyone started yelling and gasping, and I was ordered to stay still.

'Don't move, Paris, don't move . . .' said the anaesthetist, while the poor woman was wheeled out and a replacement was drafted in. I'm told the midwife made a full recovery. I'm sure I remember this story better than she does!

The fact that all my births have been induced means I've never experienced any unexpected labour pains, or any sudden breaking of waters. I've heard many stories of mothers being taken by surprise on buses or in supermarkets, but I'm glad to say that's never happened to me. I've been lucky to have had had six straightforward births, in spite of the cholestasis diagnosis. Athena's health problems were traumatic beyond belief but they didn't come to light until after the delivery, which itself went as planned.

And while I can't praise the medical teams enough – the care I receive from midwives and consultants is incredible – I'm usually keen to leave the hospital sooner rather than later. The length of time I've had to stay has varied between babies, but I'm usually home, safe and sound, within a day or two. Walking into the house with my newborn, wrapped up snugly in their little car seat, is such a lovely thing to do. Even sweeter is the moment we introduce the baby to their older brothers and sisters, who will literally jump for joy. But although I'm brimming with happiness – as is Tyson – I cross that threshold without any illusions. While this marks the start of an exciting new chapter, it's then that the hard work *really* starts.

Chapter Three

MAM KNOWS BEST

Becoming a parent can be incredibly daunting. I know just how scary it feels to enter that unknown territory, constantly worrying whether you're doing the right thing for your bundle of joy. However, as the years have passed – and my brood has grown – that fear factor has faded. Nowadays, when I welcome a new baby into the family fold, I'm much better at trusting my own instincts and making my own decisions. I've realised I can watch every parenting show on TV – and listen to every piece of advice from friends – but, at the end of the day, the person who best knows my child is *me.*

Prior to having my own kids, I'd hardly had any experience with tiny babies. When I was younger most of my close relatives lived far away, either down south or up north, and the kids I looked after on Tilts Farm tended to be from toddler age upwards. Before having Venezuela, I'd only ever changed one single nappy, my cousin Levi's, and made such a hash of it that my Aunt Romain had to shove me to one side and take over. So I arrived at parenting fairly unknowing, carrying the same worries and concerns as most new mothers.

When Tyson and I first brought Venezuela home from hospital, in September 2009, we were living in a rural part of Lancashire, next to a house owned by Tyson's Uncle Hughie (who also trained him at that time). Our trailer was based in his backyard, adjacent to a garage that had been converted into a boxing gym for Tyson's fitness and sparring sessions.

I remember lifting my daughter out of the car, all comfy and snug in her baby seat, and a voice in my head saying, *You're a parent now, Paris. This is serious stuff. From now on, this little person depends on you . . .*

The sense of responsibility was overwhelming for a nineteen-year-old. I'd spent nearly nine months gearing myself up for this moment, but nothing quite prepared me for the feelings of self-doubt as the reality of parenthood set in. Venezuela looked so tiny and fragile, and I hoped and prayed I'd be up to the job. I think Tyson felt the same. Until then, our day-to-day life had revolved around his boxing career, but now we had someone else as the centre of our focus for a while.

It took me two or three weeks to build up my confidence, and to stop treating my daughter like she was a china doll. I had so much to learn from scratch, but after a while I was changing nappies and sterilising bottles like I was on autopilot. Some things took a little longer to master, though. I remember trying to bath Venezuela at Mam's house and bursting into tears because I couldn't control all the writhing and wriggling. She was like a slippery little eel.

'I can't even bath my own baby,' I wailed. 'I don't deserve to be a mother . . .'

'These things take time, Paris. It all comes with practice,' Mam said, reassuringly, before showing me how to support the baby safely.

I soon settled into a proper routine, though, helped by the fact I was blessed with a model child. Little did I know that my firstborn would end up being the best behaved of all my babies. Not all of them would be so easy to manage, especially Little Tyson, whose unsettled sleeping and early-hours bawling would give me plenty of interrupted nights.

Venezuela was as good as gold during the day – she only ever cried when tired or hungry – and she was such a heavy sleeper at night. She used to have her last bottle at midnight and sometimes wouldn't stir again until 6 a.m. I had always been a night owl and would often be wide awake for hours, drinking coffee and watching DVDs while Venezuela contentedly snoozed in the crib beside me. Sometimes she slept so soundly I had to give her a gentle poke to check she was still breathing. Luckily, my ability to manage on a few hours of sleep meant I could usually function well the following day.

As for night feeds and day feeds, I've always bottle-fed my babies, from Venezuela to the present day. That's the choice I've made because it's worked out best for me, for a number of reasons, including the fact that Tyson and I can take turns with the bottle, especially in the middle of the night. Well, that's the plan. With the first two or three babies, asking Tyson to do his fair share was often more trouble than it was worth. I'd sleepily pass him the bottle, only to receive a barrage of questions like 'How much milk do I need, Paris? Can you pass me the bib? How do you wind her?'

Eventually I gave in and took over, realising it was far quicker and easier to do it myself. Things have improved over time, though, as Tyson has gained more experience as a parent. With our youngest three children, he's become much more helpful with bottle feeds, especially the 6 a.m. shift (often because he's up early anyway, preparing for his morning run or training session).

Feeding a baby is one of those 'each to their own' situations and you'll never find me lecturing or judging another mother for the personal decision she has reached. We all have varying ideas and opinions but, as long as a child is healthy and well, I don't see any issue. As with many aspects of parenting, there's no absolute right or wrong. Most parents instinctively know what's best for them and their baby.

My first experience of motherhood certainly taught me how to get organised. Due to the nature of Tyson's work (with his boxing career on the rise, he was often away at training camp), I knew Venezuela and I would be alone for a lot of the time so I had to become incredibly self-reliant, very fast. When Tyson was on the other side of the world for two months, I learned to plan ahead and psych myself up for the challenge. I always thought everything through in advance rather than doing stuff at the last minute. Fail to prepare, prepare to fail, as the saying goes. If I was going for a morning shop in Lancaster, for instance, I'd pack the baby bag the night before, double-checking it contained the usual nappies, bibs, baby wipes and muslin squares, alongside the all-important change of clothing. Sick and poop would feature a lot in those early days, of course.

Living in a trailer when Venezuela was tiny helped me become very disciplined. Living next to Uncle Hughie's house, rather than a Traveller site, meant I couldn't call upon any other mothers for help or advice. Being messy and disorganised in such a confined space is a recipe for disaster, and you need a good system in place (particularly so when there's a baby in the family). The absence of running water means you have to get supplies from outdoors – it's a very old-fashioned, back-to-basics way of life – so if you want to wash your dishes, fill a kettle or bath the baby, you have to do it in a timely manner.

Also, whenever the trailer door is opened a huge draught comes in, so you need to ensure that it's locked for twenty minutes while you bath or dress the baby. So as not to disturb us, I'd tell Tyson to come home from training at a specific time. Being this regimented definitely stood me in good stead for the future. I've always run a very tight ship at home, whether in a little trailer or a big house. With so many children around, life can be chaos – a perpetual hive of noise and activity – but I'd describe it as *organised* chaos. It may not always look that way from the outside but, make no mistake, I'm always in control.

* * *

Although I consider myself a pretty independent and self-sufficient person, I've learned to accept outside help and support when I need it, especially when I've got a newborn to care for. There's a lot of information to absorb in those first few months, none more so than the contents of the Little Red Book that every parent is given at the baby clinic, which monitors your little one's development. I always feel so proud when the graphs and charts confirm they're making good progress and hitting the right milestones. Being told by a clinician that you're doing a great job is a nice pat on the back.

Decent advice from an NHS health visitor can be invaluable, too, whether it's suggesting different feeding techniques or discussing your baby's ideal sleep position. But things aren't always straightforward. In the past, I've been advised to encourage my little ones to sleep on their backs, but at least a couple of them – Venezuela and Little Tyson – insisted on rolling onto their sides, no matter how much I tried to coax them back. In the end I just allowed them to sleep the way they wanted. Sometimes you just have to go with the flow and trust your instinct, even if you find it hard to go against the 'official' advice.

And – this is important – I've learned not to feel under pressure to be the perfect mother whenever a healthcare worker calls by. With my first two babies, Venezuela and Prince, I often felt my parenting skills were under scrutiny (which really wasn't the case) and would bend over backwards to emphasise how well I was coping, even if I happened to be struggling that particular day. This desire to impress meant that, before any visit, I'd clean the kitchen from top to bottom, dress the baby in their smartest outfit and ensure my hair and make-up were immaculate.

'I'm coping well, I'm on top of everything . . .' was the message I was trying to convey, although I shouldn't have felt the need to do this. Health visitors exist to help you, not judge you. If you're having a tough time, as many new parents do, they'd much rather you be honest. It wasn't until Baby Three came along – Little Tyson – that the penny finally dropped. I didn't need to pretend that everything was fine and dandy. I remember being visited one morning and answering the door in my pyjamas, feeling totally exhausted, aware that there were a couple of bottles in the kitchen that still hadn't been made up. But I was happy to explain to the health visitor that baby Tyson had kept me up all night, and that I was planning to sort the bottles – and then take a nap – when he had his next sleep. She was totally sympathetic, of course, and knew I was doing my best.

In my experience, health visitors (and GPs, if you see one) are as focused on the mother's well-being as the baby's. Pregnancy and birth can have a huge effect upon your health, emotionally as well as physically, and that can never be underestimated. Your body has gone through so much in such a short timeframe and, with your hormones going haywire, getting through those early days of motherhood can be difficult even with good-natured babies.

I'm fortunate to have never suffered from serious post-natal depression but there have been times, usually a few days after giving birth, when I've felt tearful and down in the dumps (often referred to as 'baby blues'). These are perfectly normal emotions to experience, and these days I won't brush them under the carpet. If I'm feeling low I'll discuss it with my health visitor, my mam or my husband. Witnessing Tyson's own mental health issues back in 2015 taught me the value of being honest and talking things through. I was expecting Valencia at the peak of his depressive illness, which was a very challenging time for a mam-to-be, as you can imagine. Tyson was so unwell that he barely registered I was having a baby, and it was hard for me not to feel a little neglected.

Back then I chose not to seek help and support from other people, though, because I was embarrassed about the whole situation and thought I could handle things myself. I felt I was a burden, when I truly wasn't. In hindsight, I wish I'd opened up to my loved ones instead of trying to be a martyr and struggling alone. When Mam or my friends Shannon or Cathy offered their help – which they did, frequently – I should have taken them up on it. They'd sensed I was struggling, even though I'd not explicitly come out with it, and said things like, 'Let me come over, Paris, I'll have the kids for twenty minutes.'

This would have eased so many of my worries and anxieties, at such a crucial time in my life. But instead I tried to soldier on, paint a smile on my face and put my best foot forward. Thankfully, Valencia arrived safe and well but, unlike the others, it wasn't a particularly happy or relaxing pregnancy. So here's the moral of the story: if the hand of help is extended when you're drowning, grab it. Yank it off. Let yourself be rescued.

In other areas of my life, my mother was always a good source of strength and advice. This was certainly the case when Tyson and I temporarily moved to Manchester to be close to his training gym, a few months after Venezuela was born. I felt very lonely and isolated over there – I had no friends or family nearby – and whenever Mam visited from Doncaster she'd always urge me to get outdoors with the baby rather than cocooning myself inside. Sitting in all day with a baby, staring at the same four walls, would send me stir-crazy, she told me. A walk to the park, a trip into town or a stop-off in a café would provide a good blast of fresh air and a welcome change of scenery. And she was right.

My mother's pearls of wisdom continue to resonate, even now. 'Don't let the baby hold you back,' she'd tell me, a great believer that having a child shouldn't prevent you from enjoying your usual active life. 'Don't get baby fever' is another of her sayings. In her opinion, it's always a good idea to have a decent gap before planning your next child, so as not to overstretch yourself. I listened to her wisdom with my first three kids, although it admittedly took me longer than I hoped to fall pregnant with Little Tyson, who is four years younger than Prince.

But I wasn't so cautious with my most recent three. Valencia, Adonis and Athena were all born very close together (I know; that's *serious* baby fever). I still catch Mam's eyebrows rising in a 'told you so ...' manner when she watches my youngest trio running me ragged. But she knows I wouldn't change them for the world, no matter how small the age gap.

As well as Mam, I'm lucky to be able to count on the support of Tyson. There's nothing more important to him than our children – our harrowing experience with Athena underlined that – and he'll do anything for them. Luckily for me, he's a very hands-on father. Most mornings he'll get up early to wake the kids, before helping me with the mammoth task of getting them all washed, dressed and fed before 8.30 a.m. He'll then take them to school or nursery (all except Venezuela, who's home-educated by a tutor), honking our Ford Transit's horn until all four are present, correct and ready to go. He'll sometimes do the afternoon school run, too, and will help out at teatime (as in controlling the kids rather than cooking the food). By seven o'clock Tyson often has his feet up, watching TV, so it's usually my responsibility to get the kids into their pyjamas and read them bedtime stories. I don't mind, though; for me it's one of the nicest jobs of the day.

When I'm lucky to have him at home, in those periods between fights, Tyson and I divide up the parenting duties quite well. I generally do most of the practical stuff – the nappy-changing, the mealtimes, the bath-and-bed routine – whereas he'll devote more energy to keeping the children entertained. He encourages the kids to keep active – as a sportsman, it's in his blood – and will often take the younger ones to the park, or the older ones for a country walk or a coastal bike ride. If we're spending the weekend at home you'll find him outside in the garden, kicking a football with Prince, Little Tyson, Valencia and Adonis (all proudly sporting their Manchester United shirts) or, if the weather's bad, he'll be indoors organising board games or video games. Whenever we're abroad he'll gladly take three or four of the kids to the beach, jumping waves or playing ball, while I stay at the poolside with the toddlers.

Yet, while he's brilliant at keeping them occupied, Tyson will be the first to admit that he doesn't cope well with the children en masse. Since he's frequently away from home, I've become used to looking after all six of them – I pretty much take it in my stride these days – but it's too much like hard work for my husband. Sometimes he has no choice – if I'm feeling unwell, for instance, or if I'm appearing on *Loose Women* – but it's usually under duress. You can literally see the sweat pouring down his forehead when I return to take them off his hands.

'Thank God you're here,' he'll say.

'Welcome to my world, Tyson,' I'll reply. 'D'you need to have a lie-down in a darkened room?'

More than anything, he can't bear the noise that half a dozen children can create (and believe me, their volume levels can hit the max). It's particularly difficult if he's just returned from an overseas training camp, where everything has been calm, disciplined and organised. The chaos of family life, with kids charging around, toys being thrown about and people coming and going, is a huge contrast to the virtual isolation of the boxing gym. It always takes Tyson a while to adjust and acclimatise. But, given a bit of time and space, he eventually gets into the swing of things. And, to make things more manageable, when we're doing weekend errands or activities Tyson and I will often divide our brood in half, taking charge of either the older ones (Venezuela and Prince) or the younger ones (Valencia, Adonis and Athena). Little

Tyson's in the middle so he can tag on to either group. Having just three of them in the car or in the park does make life easier, I must admit.

I'd be the first to say that raising six children can be challenging in all sorts of ways, but in my experience the hardest thing to get right is being 'all things to everyone'. Dividing my time equally among the kids can be really tricky, but it's something I always strive to achieve. This is particularly the case when there are babies and toddlers in the house, who, quite naturally, demand more attention than the older, school-age children. But it's important they all have some individual TLC, which I think they do. I have plenty of time with them all, and I think I've got the balance about right. That's why I don't put too much pressure on myself to go out to work. If I'm asked to appear on TV shows, or give interviews, or attend product launches, and it means travelling miles away or spending time apart from my kids, I'll turn them down. Most of the work I do, other than the odd trip to London, is home-based and takes place within school hours or after the children's bedtime. My family always comes first, but I know I'm lucky to be able to make that choice.

One of my toughest parenting challenges arose when Adonis came on the scene, since I already had Little Tyson (aged two) and Valencia (aged one) tugging on each trouser leg. So that meant three bottles, three car seats, three sets of nappies and three changes of clothing whenever we set foot out of the house. Some days it became absolutely exhausting. My mam helped me out a lot, bless her – she probably spent more time in Lancashire than Yorkshire in those days – and Tyson did his bit, too. He'd get up in the early hours to prepare Adonis' bottle and, if I ever started to flag during the day, he'd take the trio off my hands for a couple of hours, sometimes driving them over to Manchester to see his family.

At one stage, when I was feeling particularly frazzled, I did toy with the idea of employing a nanny. My chosen candidate came over to see the children in their home environment one afternoon and within hours she'd emailed me to politely rule herself out. The kids had been especially wild that day, so I could hardly blame her. That said, I've since found a kind and caring babysitter, Gabby, who's a godsend (especially when Tyson is training abroad) and who offers me a helping hand with the younger ones when I need it. The children love Gabby, and having her around makes it much easier to share myself equally among them, instead of being pulled from pillar to post. Parenting experts often agree that one of the most important things you can give your children is time, and I think I've achieved a pretty good blend so far. Nowadays, I never feel torn between the kids, or full of guilt that one is receiving more attention than the other. At some point in the week, no matter how busy I am, they'll all get their little piece of me.

*   *   *

Our kids get along with each other really well. It's a good job, because family life would be a nightmare if they didn't. Like most brothers and sisters, they have occasional disputes – usually over toys or video games – but, aside from that perfectly normal sibling rivalry, they all love each other very much. The eldest two, Venezuela and Prince, are extremely close and will often go swimming together, or pop to the corner shop to get me a few items. And I'll often find the younger children sitting round the table with their colouring books, or in the garden scrambling around on the climbing frame. It's so lovely to see them having fun together. The kids are friends as well as siblings – there's always someone to chat to, or play with – and I'd definitely say that's one of the benefits of having a large family.

Not only that, now that Venezuela and Prince are getting older and more responsible they'll often look after their younger brothers and sisters, which of course helps. Venezuela might take Athena for a walk around the garden, for instance, or Prince might teach

Adonis some football skills. It's a win-win when that happens.

My children may love spending time in each other's company, but they all have very different and distinct personalities. Tyson and I have always given them space to develop their own unique characters, because the last thing we want is a bunch of identical kids. Venezuela, for starters, is the perfect older sister. She's very grounded, with a kind heart and a gentle nature, yet – like many first-born children – is also incredibly headstrong and independent. Over the past couple of years, she's developed a really sweet bond with her baby sister, Athena, and likes to take her under her wing.

Prince (or Prince John James, to use his full name) is a big boy for a ten-year-old – he's stockily built, like his dad – and loves all types of sports. He's also thoughtful and, if he's asked to speak to camera (perhaps if we're doing a documentary), he's really articulate. Like most lads approaching their teens he can be a little bit lazy, though – he's always the last one out of bed in the morning.

There's a four-year gap between Prince and Little Tyson. As I had a few problems conceiving him, he became quite a special baby to us and – if I'm being honest with myself – I was probably guilty of mollycoddling him in the early days. As a toddler, he was a mischievous little scamp – he was forever getting into trouble – but since he's reached school age he's calmed down a lot. Being in a classroom with other children (and now having three younger siblings!) has made Little Tyson realise he's no longer the centre of attention.

Valencia, our middle daughter, is very smart, sassy and full of personality. She reminds me of myself in many ways; she knows what she wants, she hates being told what to do and she won't stand for any nonsense. She loves dressing up and playing role-play games, whether that's doctors and patients or princes and princesses, and often ropes in her brothers to take part.

Adonis gets the accolade for being the noisiest child in the family, which is quite something; none of the Fury kids are exactly shrinking violets! He was the youngest of five for a year or so, before Athena came along, so I think he felt the need to yell and holler to get attention. He's a little sweetheart, though – he's a gorgeous-looking boy who can make your heart melt – and is completely obsessed with anything related to Spider-Man (his last birthday party was themed accordingly).

Athena, the baby of the bunch, is a spirited, strong-willed little girl who likes to get what she wants, even if it means by force (trying to stop her grabbing and snatching is a work in progress!). She fought for her life after she was born, of course, so this may well account for her feisty character; it's as if she's trying to prove her strength and resilience. The fact she's very bright and alert is such a relief, considering the trauma she endured.

You never know where your attention is going to be thrown next with six children, from babies to teens. They all have their different needs, whether it's Athena crying for her bottle, Adonis demanding I build him a Lego castle or Venezuela using me as a sounding board for some friendship issues. But I can safely say (and Mam and Dad did warn me!) that the most difficult stage to manage is the teenage phase. It's a whole new ball game. I appreciate that raising babies and toddlers can be emotionally and physically demanding – Athena and Adonis are still quite needy – but at least I'm in full control when they're so little. I can feed them, wash them, push them along in their prams and put them to bed, while overseeing their lives 24/7.

Then, when they're aged between six and eleven, you enter the most straightforward parenting phase (well, it is in my experience!). While the children still remain under your rule, they are less clingy, more self-reliant and able to make their own entertainment. There's no need to constantly hover over them and, as their social skills improve, and their sense of humour develops, they can be really good fun to be around. Little Tyson is a prime example of that. He's always making us laugh with his daft jokes and silly pranks.

Then come the tricky teens. Venezuela is now thirteen, with Prince following closely behind. While it's normal and healthy for young people to crave more independence, and to socialise with friends in the wider world, it can be a worrying state of affairs for us parents. You can spend years guiding your precious kids through life, teaching them how to behave and how to stay safe, but gradually loosening those apron strings can be so difficult. When they're off your radar you find yourself fretting about everything, from crossing the road properly to attending teenage parties.

Don't get me wrong, my eldest daughter is a really level-headed girl, with a great set of friends, but that doesn't stop me feeling anxious whenever she leaves the house. I often find myself repeating the words my mam used to say to me back when I was a teenager.

'I totally trust *you*, Paris,' she'd say, 'but I don't always trust other people. Not everyone's as sensible as you.'

Parenting a teenager is like performing a balancing act: on the one hand you're keen to give them some freedom, yet on the other hand you want them to stay safe. Tyson and I find ourselves striking lots of compromise deals with Venezuela. There has to be some give and take. For instance, we might allow her to attend a friend's party, on the proviso that we pick her up at 10 p.m. prompt. Or we might let her go to the cinema, as long as she's watching a film that's appropriate. I get the feeling that, however old my children are, I'll never stop worrying about them. They'll forever be my babies.

*　*　*

Tyson and I have a few golden rules when it comes to raising our kids in the right manner. First of all, we're sticklers for good social skills, particularly so in this day and age. Whether we like it or not, we live in an era where people are glued to their mobile phones, texting, messaging and posting at the expense of good old-fashioned conversation. But it's good to talk – let's be honest, Tyson and I are rarely lost for words – and we want to bring up a new generation of chatterboxes. Don't get me wrong, I'm not completely blameless – I enjoy a quick scroll through my Instagram timeline – but I try to save social media for the evening, rather than during the day when I'm with the children.

I think it's good to instil good social skills at an early age. As soon as my kids are born I start talking to them, and I give them loads of eye-to-eye contact, so they can get used to the sound of my voice and my facial expressions. As they grow older and become more alert I'll natter non-stop to them in their pushchair as I wheel them around the park, pointing out trees, birds, bicycles, whatever. It all helps to build up their vocabulary. During long car journeys the kids and I will play a game of 'spot the sheep' or 'count the lorries', just like Mam and Dad did back in the 1990s, when we travelled up to see family in Newcastle.

Listening to my children is just as important as talking to them. I like to give them the space and opportunity to tell me about their day, or to talk about what's on their mind. It can get really crazy when I do the afternoon school run, though. Once they've piled into the van, Prince, Little Tyson, Valencia and Adonis will all talk at once, ten to the dozen, desperate to tell me about what they've learned in the classroom and who they've played with in the playground. They'll fight to get their voices heard, and it inevitably descends into a massive, deafening row.

'Valencia, *I'm* talking, *I'm* talking . . .'

'No, Prince, it's my turn . . .'

'EVERYONE STOP SHOUTING!!!'

'But you're the loudest of us all, Adonis . . .'

I'll then have to intervene to calm everyone down.

'Woah, woah, one at a time, you noisy bunch . . . right, you go first, Prince, then the rest of you can follow . . .'

So I'll hear all about learning backstroke in the swimming lesson . . . receiving a Good Behaviour star from the teacher . . . eating a yummy school dinner of fish and

chips . . . playing a great skipping game at break-time . . .
and so on. It can be pretty trivial stuff in the scheme of
things but I love to listen to their chatter, especially if
they're really excited and enthusiastic about something.
It also gets them into the habit of opening up about their
thoughts and feelings, something that Tyson – in light of
his own mental health issues – is very keen to encourage. He spent years suppressing his emotions, and he'd
hate his own children to be in a similar position.

Interacting well with people in the wider world is
important, too, and helping children with their communi-
cation skills can stand them in good stead for later life. My
parents taught me how to speak easily to people from all
backgrounds; in fact, as a teenager I used to help out in
my dad's jewellery shop, and dealing with customers and
answering phone calls did wonders for my confidence
levels and my conversational skills. And, now I'm a mother
myself, I'm taking a leaf out of Mam and Dad's book. I
don't want my kids to be wallflowers.

'There's your money, go to the till, pay for your toy and
talk to the lady,' I'll say, or 'Don't just take the letter from
the postman. Have a chat. Ask him how his day's going.'

If we're in a restaurant, I'll ask the children to order
their own food from the menu, to be courteous to the
waiting staff and to make conversation with one another
round the table. And whenever we're attending a social

gathering I'll ask them to chat politely with other guests. I'll tell them not to just answer Yes or No if they're asked a question, and not to shrug their shoulders or mumble, 'um, I don't know' like I've seen other kids do. Instead, they must make the effort to strike up a conversation, always making sure they ask about the other person as well. Even if someone asks, 'How's your dad?' (as many people do, because of who Tyson is), I tell my kids to simply reply, 'He's very well, thank you' rather than just ignoring them.

Being polite makes all the difference and reflects well on them and us. When Little Tyson was about three, I remember him getting on to a plane and saying to one of the cabin crew, 'Hello lady, can I have a can of Coke?' He wasn't too young to be reminded that polite little boys say 'please' . . .

Tyson and I both believe that having good manners and showing respect is paramount in life. It's another one of our golden rules. We don't tolerate rudeness and always expect the kids to treat people with kindness and courtesy, whether it's friends, family or others. Give or take the odd tantrum and meltdown from the younger kids – usually in shops or restaurants! – I'm very proud of the way they conduct themselves. Complete strangers often come over to compliment me on the children's good behaviour, which is always music to my ears.

However, being out and about with a sporting super-star – especially one as distinctive-looking as Tyson – isn't always easy for the children. He attracts so much attention, and more often than not will be mobbed by fans requesting selfies and autographs. Other celebrities can avoid being spotted by just whacking on a baseball cap and a pair of shades, but that never does the trick for Tyson. Most people can recognise his six-foot-nine frame a mile off.

On the whole, the kids cope brilliantly with all the attention; to them it's commonplace, I suppose, and they've been taught to stay calm and stay by our sides at all times. There have been occasions when it's all got a bit too much, though. While most fans behave very respectfully towards us when we're going about our daily business, others can overstep the mark. Some members of the public get giddy when they catch sight of Tyson, and seem to lose their heads, pointing and yelling in our faces and not thinking twice about disrupting our family time in order to get to their hero. A couple of years ago, Valencia was knocked to the ground while someone tried to take a selfie with Tyson. Luckily she wasn't hurt, but it acted as a wake-up call for us. Nowadays, we often have to employ bodyguards if we're all together in public. Our children's safety and security is paramount.

I must point out that we're rarely bothered in Morecambe, though. We're part of the local fabric in our home town, and the fact we're treated like ordinary residents is one of the reasons we've chosen to raise our family here. We can do the weekly supermarket shop, or go for a Sunday pub lunch, and not face any hassle whatsoever. It's only when we venture out of Lancashire that we feel under the spotlight.

* * *

Appreciating the value of money, and being grateful for your possessions, is another golden rule in our family. Tyson's boxing success may have given us financial security, but we make it clear to our children that it should never be taken for granted. They realise that, in their dad's case, good fortune didn't just land in his lap; it took years of blood, sweat and tears for Tyson to become world champion. And while we could easily bankroll our children for life, we'd prefer not to pursue that route. As far as we're concerned, life isn't a free ride, and money can't buy you happiness. With that in mind, we're trying to guide our children towards having their own aims, goals and objectives, rather than sitting on their backsides and relying on others. Shaping their own careers and earning their own money will give them far more personal satisfaction, in our opinion.

'Find something you have a passion for, and build things from there,' I'll say, often using my short but sweet stint as a beauty therapist as an example. Not only was it a job I loved to bits, it taught me a lot about self-worth and self-sufficiency.

I try not to be overly flash with money in front of the children. I appreciate I'm able to afford the finer things in life but, in saying that, I'm still keen to teach the children about saving money and managing budgets. I still shop at the cheaper supermarkets and discount stores and, just as Mam did with me, I'll teach my kids money-saving tips like opting for own brands or buying in bulk. I still enjoy sifting through a sale rail – which makes Venezuela cringe – and can't resist a good bargain at Primark or Poundland.

Sometimes I purposely don't give the children what they want, even though I know (and they know) that we can afford it. Quite simply, I don't want them to assume we have a bottomless pit of money.

'Mam, can I have two pounds for the corner shop?' Prince might ask.

'No,' I'll reply, shaking my head. 'You've already had money today. Once it's gone, it's gone.'

'Aww, please . . .'

79

'I said *no*, Prince.'

In terms of possessions, I don't think my kids are treated any differently to their friends or cousins. They don't get showered with gifts throughout the year, and certainly don't get anything more fancy than their pals (except Venezuela, perhaps, now that she's getting into clothes and fashion). We certainly don't buy them the new Manchester United kit or the latest Disney play set as soon as they're released in the shops. If anything, they'll accuse me of being unfair for not buying them something their friend already has.

'Aww, why can't I have that PlayStation game too, Mam?'

'You'll just have to wait, won't you? Christmas isn't too far away . . .'

Ultimately, Tyson and I are bringing up our six children to be as grounded as possible. We know our life isn't typical – being a Fury puts us all in the spotlight – but we're doing our utmost to instil the right values and principles just as we had them instilled as kids. When Tyson and I were young, we were taught that we couldn't always have everything we wanted. Money didn't grow on trees; it was earned by the hard work of others. That's the sort of message we're trying to push, and only time will tell if we get it right. Away from the glitz and glamour of Tyson's professional life, we're just dealing as best we can with ordinary issues, and trying to do the right thing, wanting our kids to be as well-equipped as possible for whatever life has in store for them.

CHAPTER FOUR

TANTRUMS, TRIUMPHS AND TROUBLESHOOTING

LET'S BE HONEST: the perfect parent doesn't exist. It's a myth. While we do our utmost to be good mams and dads, and raise our kids in the correct manner, we can't be expected to get everything right. Making mistakes is totally normal in the grand scheme of things – we're only human – and at some point we'll all mess up. I, for one, am never taken in by those sugary-sweet, picture-perfect families portrayed in TV adverts or on social media. They bear no relation to real life. Everyone has chinks in their armour, no matter who they are. Parenting is a patchwork quilt of good days (when all goes to plan) and bad days (when all goes to pot). 'Life isn't all sunshine and rainbows.'

It took me a while to figure this out, though. When I was younger, and new to motherhood, I put far too much pressure on myself. I tried so hard to be the greatest mam in the world – I felt I had something to prove, and people to impress – and would become incredibly upset if I thought I'd got things wrong. When I couldn't get the hang of bathing Venezuela, for example, or struggled to soothe Little Tyson to sleep, I thought I was failing as a parent. However, as time went by, and I got into the swing of things, I stopped trying to achieve perfection. I wasn't SuperMam. I accepted that my best was good enough, no matter if there were a few bumps and blips along the way. My children were healthy, happy and cared-for, and that was more important than anything.

So if I have an epic parenting 'fail' nowadays I don't beat myself up. Instead, I hold up my hands and say, 'OK, I got that wrong . . . I'll do better next time.' I've decided to learn from my mistakes instead of dwelling on them.

* * *

I love my children dearly, and am extremely proud of all six, but I'll be the first to admit their behaviour can be challenging. Daily toddler tantrums and teenage sulks are common in our household. In fact, I'd politely suggest that any parent who claims their son or daughter is as good as gold, from dawn 'til dusk, from Monday morning to Sunday night, isn't telling the truth. That's just not how it happens. Some of my kids have been easier to manage than others. Venezuela was a dream baby and toddler (she's making up for it now she's a teenager) but all six have tested my patience at times, and have needed reining in, good and proper.

When it comes to disciplining the children, Tyson and I are on the same page . . . well, almost. Fundamentally, we are bringing up our kids to be kind, polite and respectful and we won't stand for any poor behaviour. But, that being said, there's definitely a Good Cop/Bad Cop routine in our household (Tyson being the softie and me being the toughie), which means I dish out most of the time-outs and tellings-off. I'm much better at setting boundaries for the children, and sticking to them, so they know when they've crossed the line. Tyson, on the other hand, is far more likely to let them get away with things, or cave in to their demands. He often takes the easy option; anything for a quiet life. So if I'm paying for something in our corner shop, for example, and Valencia and Adonis put bags of sweets on the counter without asking, I'll make them put them back on the shelves. They might cry, shout and stamp their feet but – out of principle – I'll always stick to my guns. However, if the same scenario happens with Tyson, he'll immediately give in, just to keep the peace. It can be so infuriating.

'Those two have just cost me an extra tenner because they had a meltdown,' he'll moan when he returns from the store, laden with Haribos.

'Well, more fool you, Tyson,' I'll reply. 'You're the adult here. Put your foot down.'

I couldn't care less about giving my children a public telling-off – passers-by can say and think what they like – but, whenever he's out and about, Tyson hates making a scene if the kids kick up a fuss. In fairness to him, he does have a valid reason for not wishing to draw attention to himself. The world is full of people carrying camera phones, including some who'll film anything (yes, even Tyson Fury trying to control his kids in a sweet shop) if it means going viral on social media. So I do have some sympathy, and understand why he occasionally lets the children off the hook, but I also know it suits him to avoid any tantrums.

In the aftermath of a big fight, my husband is even more of a pushover. When he's shut away in his training camp he misses the family so much, and he can't wait to get home to Morecambe to catch up with us all and make up for lost time. The last thing he wants to do is get on the kids' wrong side, even if it means overruling me. I might tell them they're not allowed to play on their hand-held devices until after teatime, for example, but once I turn my back, Tyson will hand them over. The children know he's an easy touch, compared with me, and will often take full advantage. It drives me mad, I admit, but we don't have stand-up rows about it. Sometimes it's not worth the hassle, especially if it's at the end of a long, tiring day. But the next time we're out at a restaurant, and Adonis refuses to be parted from his Nintendo DS, I'll shrug my shoulders and give Tyson a look as if to say, 'Well, don't blame me . . .'

The girls in particular can wind Tyson round their little fingers. He's soft as putty with his beloved daughters. One evening, Venezuela was going to her primary school leaving party and came downstairs in a party dress, teamed with a giant pair of my designer six-inch heels (we have the same shoe size these days).

'You are *not* wearing those shoes, Venezuela,' I scolded. 'They're far too high for you, and you can hardly walk in them.'

'Aw, please, Mam,' she whined. 'All the girls will be wearing heels. I'll look stupid in flats.'

Then I thought I'd be clever by asking my daughter to seek her dad's opinion. I was pretty sure that Tyson would agree with me, perhaps not so keen to see his little girl wobbling around in such grown-up shoes. If he said she could wear them, I'd give her my approval. So she went upstairs to ask him the question – I think he was having a nap – and within a minute she came tottering down the stairs again.

'Dad said *yes!*' she said, smiling from ear to ear. 'He said it's a special occasion.'

'Typical,' I tutted. 'Yet again, he's the good cop, and I'm the bad cop . . .'

But Tyson isn't always a goody-two-shoes. One of my biggest bugbears, behaviour-wise, is his usage of foul language in front of the children. I'm not a person who swears a lot – I share my mam's dislike of it – and bad words rarely pass my lips (and even then, it's usually when I've been pushed to the limit). I can't say the same for Tyson, sadly. Ever since I've known him he's been a potty-mouth, like many people in the sporting world I suppose. He tries his best to speak nicely in front of the children, but his bad language is so ingrained he'll inadvertently drop a swear-word into a conversation, or will start effing and jeffing on the phone to his brother or a boxing pal.

And while the older children realise this is impolite and inappropriate, the younger children may not, and have been known to repeat certain words and phrases for the fun of it. It's a constant battle, one that's often resolved with a time-out or a PlayStation ban (the kids, not Tyson). My husband knows it maddens me, however, and is forever apologising when he slips up, but he knows he needs to clean up his act. He's finally learned not to drop the F-bomb on live television (it only took him ten years to get right), so I still live in hope.

'If you can go on *Good Morning Britain* and talk sweetly with Susanna Reid, you can do the same with us, too,' I once said to him. I shan't tell you what his reply was.

And while I'm quick to chastise the kids if they get something wrong – like using bad language – I'm also the first to reward good behaviour. It's important to recognise the positives as well as the negatives. If, for instance, Prince receives a school certificate that praises his attitude in class, I'll make a fuss of him and offer him a treat. I might let him choose his favourite comic or chocolate bar or, alternatively, give him a fiver to spend in the amusement arcade on the seafront. And if Venezuela works particularly hard with her tutor one afternoon, or offers to help look after Athena, I'll show my gratitude by taking her into town to get her nails done or buying her a new T-shirt from TK Maxx. Yet these acknowledgements don't always need to be tangible. Sometimes a one-to-one chat at the kitchen table, emphasising how pleased you are, can mean the world to a child and can really help their self-esteem. Not only that, it can encourage more of the same behaviour. I used to love making my mam and dad happy and proud, and I hope my kids feel the same.

* * *

When the younger kids have a meltdown at home – perhaps they're refusing to share a toy with their brother or sister – I try to tackle it in my own way (but not always successfully, I admit). Initially, I attempt to gently reason with them, explaining why they should behave nicely. If they don't respond to that, and their shouting and screaming begins to upset their siblings, I'll then remove them from the situation and put them somewhere safe, like their bedroom, where they can take some time to chill out. I always leave the door ajar (so they don't feel as though they're being locked in) and perhaps hand them a comforting cuddly toy, or put on their favourite DVD. More often than not, after five or ten minutes of boring isolation their temper will cool and they'll come back downstairs, and will be ready to play nicely.

Sometimes, though, they refuse to calm down and Bad Cop might have to make an appearance. Yelling at my kids is always a last resort – I don't enjoy doing it – but occasionally it's the only thing that works. And boy, can I shout. I can project right across the room like a school-teacher. Even Tyson, who has a voice like a foghorn, complains about my volume levels.

'Paris, d'you have to be quite so loud, for goodness' sake?'

'Yes, I do, actually . . . no one takes a blind bit of notice otherwise.'

Trying to get six kids out of the house can be a very stressful experience. I'll start out by politely asking them to put on their coats, shoes, hats and gloves. Then I'll advise them a little more forcefully. And if by the third request they're still dragging their feet, dithering about or totally ignoring me, I'll erupt like a volcano.

'Get . . . your . . . things . . . on . . . *NOW!!!*'

Operation Fishwife is not my preferred solution, but it usually does the trick. Like most modern-day parents, I don't believe in smacking children in *any* circumstances – even as a shock tactic, maybe to stop a child from running into the road – so, when it comes to controlling my kids, sometimes only a good yell will do.

Coping with temper tantrums, particularly in public areas, can be another serious test of a parent's resolve. I know I'm not alone in having to deal with them in restaurants, playgrounds and supermarkets. All my kids have kicked off, big style, at some point or other, the flashpoint age usually being between two and six years old. As I write, young Adonis is going through his peak tantrum phase.

We recently had an epic, thirty-minute meltdown in Asda, just because he'd spotted a big blue teddy on the shelves that I refused to put in the trolley. He screamed uncontrollably as I went up and down the aisles. I tried to calm him, I tried to cajole him and I tried to ignore him, but nothing worked. I even lifted him out of the trolley, crouching down low, holding his hands and talking to him at eye-level like I'd once seen on a 'good parenting' TV show. When that went pear-shaped, I ended up giving Adonis a bag of pickled onion Monster Munch as a distraction, although he was still sobbing about the flippin' blue bear when we got to the till. The only upside was that he tired himself out so much, he dropped off in the car and slept for most of the afternoon. Sometimes you have to be thankful for small mercies.

Patience is an essential quality when you're a parent, especially when your kids play up, but I must confess that mine is wearing thinner by the day. In the early days of motherhood, I had it in abundance. With only Venezuela and Prince to look after, time was plentiful and I could spend hours playing in the park, rustling up fancy meals and reading them long bedtime stories. I was like Morecambe's version of Mary Poppins. But with the arrival of more kids, and the upsurge in stress levels, my patience has been downgraded to 'tolerance'. My fuse is definitely shorter these days. Maybe peace and calm will return to my life once the kids have grown up.

Venezuela and Prince – my elder pair – passed the tantrum stage many years ago. However, they can still challenge me in other ways. They're both really good kids, but as they grow in confidence they occasionally cross the line, perhaps giving me some backchat if they can't get their own way. Venezuela's phone usage is a case in point. It's a modern-day dilemma that may chime with parents of similarly aged children. When my daughter turned twelve I allowed her (somewhat reluctantly) to have a smartphone, in common with most of her friends. Within weeks, however, I wished I hadn't. Firstly, Tyson and I soon noticed she was spending far too much time staring at her phone and scrolling through messages. She seemed constantly distracted by her device and was barely interacting with the family.

Secondly, we were alarmed to discover Venezuela was accessing (and posting on) a certain social media site, despite being previously warned that it was strictly off-limits. Tyson and I discussed this together – luckily we were on the same page – and after dinner one night we raised these concerns with our daughter. It was important that we put on a united front, and demonstrated how serious we were. We talked things through calmly and sensibly, explaining how her detached attitude had worried us, and outlining the dangers of the internet for a young person, especially the child of a celebrity.

We told her that any online content, no matter how daft and innocent, could easily be mocked or misinterpreted, and might even be picked up by the media. Any mistakes or mishaps would be amplified – perhaps more than her friends in similar circumstances – just because of who her parents are. And we were also concerned that she'd come across some of the nasty trolls that sadly exist on the internet, who will post vile comments about me and Tyson (and, unbelievably, our kids). Any parent worth their salt would want to shield their offspring from these hurtful and harmful insults. We could do our bit by not buying tabloid newspapers, and putting parental controls on computers, but it would be much harder to control a child's phone usage.

Venezuela felt very hard done by. There were a few tears, and a few cross words – 'Why can't you be normal people?' she said – but it was eventually decided that, for her own safety and protection, her iPhone would be replaced by a basic handset without internet access. We wouldn't let her have another smartphone until she was older.

'But Mam, how am I going to message my friends?' she asked.

'You can ring them, you can text them, you can even knock on their door if you like,' I replied. 'That's what me and your dad used to do.'

After a few weeks of sulking, Venezuela accepted our decision and, much to our relief, soon returned to her happy-go-lucky self. I think she now realises that there are inevitable downsides to being the teenage child of a public figure – pressures largely related to privacy and security – but that, at the same time, the disadvantages are greatly outweighed by the advantages. I'm pretty sure Venezuela loves being a Fury, on the whole, and I hope the other children feel the same way too. They all live very privileged lives, and have seen places, met people and possessed things that other kids their age could only dream of. But Tyson and I do appreciate that our children suffer certain pressures and problems that others don't, and we do offer them our love and support when it's needed.

We also have to set a good example and practise what we preach. While the smartphone ban is in place, I'm careful to monitor my own behaviour when it comes to devices. I don't want the kids to see me glued to my phone – that would be pretty hypocritical of me – so I purposely limit my daytime usage. You'll never see me messaging or posting while I'm pushing a pram or sat in the park; I think my children deserve my full attention when we're out and about.

I also try to restrict the younger kids' access to tablets. In my experience, they can be both a help and a hindrance. When a child is whiny and grizzly it's easy and conveni-ent for parents to pacify them with their favourite cartoon on YouTube or iPlayer. I guess most of us have done it, especially when we're in restaurants or on aeroplanes, just to give us half an hour's respite. But resort to this too often, and you run the risk of a mega-meltdown when you take the tablet away, or the kids' becoming over-reliant on it at the expense of conventional, old-fashioned toys. I know Little Tyson, Valencia and Adonis would stare at screens for hours if I let them, so I'm always careful to give them a time limit, supervise what they're watching and put all the parental locks in place.

Whether us oldies like it or not, digital technology plays a massive role in kids' learning and leisure activities – it's the future – so depriving them isn't necessarily the best move. But I suppose it's down to us, as parents, to manage it sensibly. It's not always easy to find that happy medium, though.

* * *

By far the craziest time of day in the Fury household is the period between 7.30 a.m. (when my alarm goes off) and 8.30 a.m. (when Tyson drives the kids to school). It's even more frantic when my husband is away training, because I'm left to do everything single-handedly. So on those mornings I'll wake up, rub my eyes, take a deep breath, spring out of bed and prepare for an hour of chaos. Having a lie-in is never on the cards, even on

Sundays or during school holidays. I've always been an early riser. It's in my nature. I just don't see the point in stagnating under the covers if I've gone to bed at a normal time and had a decent night's sleep. The only time I ever stay in bed after eight o'clock is if I'm feeling unwell, and that (touch wood) is a rarity.

My first early-morning task is to get four drowsy children out of bed (Venezuela is home-schooled, so will usually look after baby Athena while I'm running around after the others). It remains one of life's mysteries why, at weekends, my children can be bouncing on my bed at 6 a.m., whereas each Monday morning I have to quite literally drag them out from beneath their duvets. Ten-year-old Prince is by far the laziest. Sometimes it's like trying to raise a corpse.

'Get up, Prince, it's seven thirty,' I'll say, throwing open his curtains and switching on the lights.

'Just five more minutes, please . . .' he'll groan, burying his head under the pillow.

Then I'll usher them into the bathroom to wash their faces, clean their teeth and brush their hair. I'll supervise Adonis and Valencia myself, but have to trust Prince and Little Tyson to sort themselves out and not cut any corners. I often ask the older boys to breathe in my face and, if I can't smell toothpaste, they're back in that bathroom before you can say Aquafresh.

After that, they'll return to their bedrooms to get dressed. And that's when a little prep comes in handy, courtesy of a life hack that my mother taught me. To save unnecessary hassle, I organise the children's clothes and accessories the night before. I ensure they all have clean school uniforms and underwear, which I drape at the ends of their beds so they can quickly grab them and pull them on. I have neither the time nor the patience to iron shirts or locate socks, especially first thing in the morning when I'm half asleep and my brain is hardly functioning. This system works like clockwork, even if I say so myself.

Next, the kids will run downstairs and pile into the kitchen for breakfast. They generally help themselves to whatever takes their fancy in the fridge or the cupboard, whether it's a bowl of cornflakes, a pot of yoghurt or a slice of toast. While they're eating, I'll attempt to sort out their school bags and sports kits (that's if I can find them in the first place, as they're often kicked under beds or left in the car boot). While I try to give them responsibility for their own belongings, like most kids they can be very forgetful and will often need a helping hand. No doubt residents across the Bay can hear me bawling, 'SO WHO'S GOT P.E. TODAY?' every morning.

When Tyson's at home – usually during those long-ish periods between fights – he'll do the 8.30 a.m. school run with Prince, Little Tyson and Valencia and, half an hour later, I'll do the nursery drop with Adonis. More often than not I'll do the afternoon collection, too, because it tends to clash with Tyson's daily gym session. I always breathe a sigh of relief when we can divvy things up in the morning, since doing both trips can be a real struggle. And – confession time – there have been occasions when, if I'm running *really* late, I've done the school run in my pyjamas. Come on, which mam hasn't? It's only ever as a last resort, though, and you'll never catch me getting out of the car to walk the children to the school gate (it'd be just my luck for someone to take a cheeky snapshot, and for PARIS IN HER PJs to appear in some tabloid or other). Instead, I'll park up as close as I can before telling the kids to run in by themselves.

Back at home, the after-school period is something of a free-for-all. I allow the children an hour or so to relax and let off steam, which usually means the TV being switched on and the PlayStation being powered up. At some point I'll try to cajole Prince, Valencia and Little Tyson into completing their homework before teatime but, for the eldest of the trio, this often proves to be easier said than done. Prince regularly forgets to bring his books and worksheets back home – he can also get very tired after a long school day – and as a result we've had to strike a deal with his class teacher. He now does a lot of this extra work during his morning break-time, when he's able to focus more. Valencia and Little Tyson, in contrast, don't feel quite so frazzled when they return from school, and willingly crack on with their numeracy and literacy tasks. In fact, my middle son even asked for his own homework desk for a Christmas present ... I was quite impressed by that, I must say.

I take a fairly strict, hardline approach to the kids' homework. I don't mind giving them a helping hand if they need it, but I much prefer them to figure things out themselves if they can. That way, they get used to working independently and using their own initiative. And if they forget to complete their homework, or they hand it in too late, I won't offer any wishy-washy excuses to the teacher. My kids have to be accountable for their own actions, and have to take responsibility if they slip up.

'If you've not done the work, *you* need to tell the teacher, not *me*,' I'll say.

I know I may sound harsh, but sometimes it's the wake-up call they need. More often than not, the following week's homework will be handed in on time. I'm just encouraging them to be self-reliant. They'll thank me for it one day.

*   *   *

Come what may, we always have our evening meal together, usually around six o'clock. Food is very important to the Furys, as is the chance for us to sit and chat round the table together, as a family. Once the plates have been cleared up and put away it's time for me to prepare the children for bathtime and bedtime and, if I'm lucky, look forward to a couple of hours' peace and quiet. Well that's the plan, anyway.

On a school night, Prince and Venezuela usually go up to their rooms at 8 p.m.-ish, and are allowed to watch TV for another hour or so. The little ones, who all share a big bedroom (Athena's still in with me and Tyson), have to be tucked in for 7.30 p.m. Little Tyson is currently trying to negotiate a later bedtime, though, and is also starting to ask when he can share a room with Prince (I'm standing firm at the moment, but I think his wish will be granted sooner rather than later).

When the young ones are all snug, I'll tell them a bedtime story, or listen to them read one themselves. Tyson and I have always encouraged our kids to pick up a book, whether fiction or non-fiction. It's the perfect way to develop their knowledge and imagination, although we reckon they're probably a little too young to flick through the pages of their mam and dad's bestsellers. Their current favourites include *The Gruffalo* and *Cave Baby*, both written by Julia Donaldson, which are lovely stories to read.

Once they're in the Land of Nod, all being well, it's time for me to wind down. I rarely watch television during the week (I got out of the habit when the kids came along) so, instead, I'll sit down in the kitchen or the living room with a cup of coffee. I might take the opportunity to catch up with my emails and WhatsApps, or have a quick scroll through Instagram. If Tyson's around we'll have a chat about our day (if he's away, we'll do it on the phone, or over FaceTime) and we'll maybe watch a movie together, until around 11 p.m. It's this period of calm, between the kids' bedtime and mine, that keeps me sane and stable. It allows me to relax, recharge my batteries and get my head straight before the following morning's mayhem.

Having a long and undisturbed sleep is the Holy Grail for most parents. For me and Tyson, however, this has been very hit-and-miss over the last decade or so. Fortunately, I don't need much shut-eye to function – I can easily survive on just five or six hours per night – so I don't really mind getting up in the early hours. To be honest, I'm far more concerned that my children get plenty of rest, so they can store enough energy to withstand the school day. I'm sure many teachers would agree that sleep deprivation can badly affect a pupil's ability to focus and concentrate.

My sleep pattern went totally haywire when Adonis was born, back in 2019. At that time, Valencia and Little

Tyson were still toddler age, so getting all three of them settled down for the night became a massive challenge. I didn't get a decent sleep for about four months. I was continually being woken up, whether it was giving Adonis his bottle, calming Valencia in her cot, or putting a restless Little Tyson back in bed. It could be so frustrating: as one child fell asleep, another would stir. I persevered, though, because I was determined to win the fight. I used to joke to Tyson that I was just like Ivan Drago in *Rocky IV*.

'I must *break* you . . .' I'd say to myself as I lowered Adonis into his cot for the umpteenth time.

I got there in the end, thank goodness. My first undisturbed sleep was definitely something to celebrate . . . until little Athena came along, of course.

A few years ago, Valencia developed a habit of creeping into our room in the dead of night and wriggling into bed with us, as many kids tend to do. If you're a parent – especially an exhausted one – it's so tempting to let them stay there, especially when they're so warm and cuddly. But by doing so you create a rod for your own back, and it can be extremely hard to break the cycle. That's essentially what happened with Valencia. In the end we had to adopt some strict tactics, carrying her back to her own bed even if she kicked up a stink. It wasn't easy – it took a lot of willpower on our part – but Valencia eventually got the drift and stayed put.

Touch wood, I think I've almost cracked the bedtime situation. I certainly get more sleep now than ever before. As I write, Athena's crib is still in our room, next to our bed, but luckily she sleeps very soundly. She only wakes up occasionally to ask for her bottle, which I can almost pass over with my eyes shut. Sometimes, Tyson and I will receive an early-hours visit from one of the other children (usually if they're feeling poorly or have had a nightmare), but those interruptions are becoming much less frequent. I think our younger kids have finally got the message that bedtime means bedtime.

*   *   *

While I'm more than happy to share advice and what works for me with other parents, I'll only ever do so if I'm asked outright. I'm not the sort of person who'll randomly offer their thoughts about the way a mother feeds, dresses or disciplines her kids, because I don't think it's my place to. Bringing up children is a very individual experience, and parents will inevitably have differing opinions; what works for them may not necessarily work for you, and vice versa.

However, if I was ever asked to offer one nugget of wisdom to fellow mams it would be this: go with the flow, but expect the unexpected. In other words, try to take motherhood in your stride – don't let babies hold you back – but be mindful of spanners in the works. For instance, I've had lunch gatherings with friends scuppered by a teething tot who can't stop crying, and I've had the weekly shop cut short after a call from school about a lost swimming kit. From bringing up Venezuela to Athena, I've come to realise that there's no such thing as a best-laid plan.

Accidents and ailments can disrupt things, too. Having six children means we're regular fixtures at the doctors and the dentist – earache one day, toothache the next – and I often joke to reception staff that they should cut us a special set of keys. The fact the older kids are now doing more after-school sports and activities – dance class, judo sessions and (surprise, surprise) boxing – means there's a higher likelihood of aches, scrapes and injuries. I will try my best to ferry them to all the various church halls and sports centres, but if there are any clashes (and Tyson's not around to bail me out) I often ask one of the other mams to help with a pick-up or a drop-off. I'll often do the same for them, if they're stretched one evening.

On a more serious note, however, I've experienced three very scary hospital emergencies with my children: most recently with Athena, but also with Prince and Little Tyson. When Prince was only six weeks old, he became desperately ill with severe respiratory pneumonia and was rushed to the intensive care unit at Sheffield Children's Hospital for specialist treatment. For almost a week he was unable to breathe independently – he had to be sedated and ventilated – and, at one point, he became so critically ill that Tyson and I were told to prepare for the worst.

'It's touch and go,' I remember the consultant saying. 'You may want to ask your family to come over.'

I could hardly process what I was hearing. 'You mean to say their goodbyes?'

I have awful memories of me and Tyson crying buckets, praying to God and willing our baby to pull through. Luckily, Prince managed to cling onto life – he had that Fury fighting spirit – and was soon able to come off the ventilator. He went on to make a full recovery, thank goodness, although in his younger years he was susceptible to chest infections and asthma-related issues. Luckily he's not troubled so much these days. In fact, seeing Prince now, so strong and sturdy, it's hard to believe what he went through.

A few years later, when Big Tyson was Stateside, training for his first fight with Deontay Wilder, another frightening incident took place. As Little Tyson ran from the car to the front door – we'd just collected Venezuela from dance class – he tripped up and landed on a concrete step, hitting his head and splitting it open. The cut went so deep you could see the white of his skull bone. The poor kid was screaming in pain – there was blood every-where – and the other three kids were upset, too, seeing their little brother in such a distressed state.

I felt like screaming the place down (my poor baby!) but I knew that would make the situation worse; instead, I had to stay calm and in control. And I had to think straight and act quickly. So I bundled the children straight back into the Transit, and sped over to the hospi-tal. While I was en route I rang my good friend Shannon, who lives nearby. She's a long-time friend of mine who's helped me out so much in the past, whether it's as a last-minute babysitter or a shoulder to cry on, and this was no exception. She knows I'd do the same for her, too.

'Can I come and pick you up?' I asked, trying not to cry in front of the children. 'Little Tyson's in a really bad way, and there's no way I can drag all the kids into A&E . . .'

'Don't you worry, Paris,' she said, calmly. 'I'll get my coat on.'

Shannon was able to keep the kids occupied in the car, which allowed me to stay with my son while a nurse stemmed the blood flow, treated his wound and stitched him up. Fortunately I'm not squeamish, but it was still awful to see my son suffering a fair amount of pain and discomfort. But Little Tyson was such a tough cookie that day, and I kept telling him how brave he was being in that A&E room, just like his daddy in the boxing ring. The cut was so deep it eventually needed plastic surgery to minimise the scarring, but in many ways my son was a very lucky boy. Had he landed on his eye or facial area, the outcome could have been much worse.

The emergencies involving Prince, Little Tyson and Athena have taught me a lot about myself. Apart from realising how precious my kids are – and how precious *life* is – they've shown me that I can cope in a time of crisis. Once my adrenalin takes over, and my maternal instincts kick in, I can handle any drama. Sometimes I cast my mind back to those terrifying moments when my kids were at risk, and wonder how I managed to stay so strong and keep myself together. But I somehow did. In times of trouble, I'm like a lioness. I'll do anything and everything to protect my little cubs.

If we're all out together, for instance, I've always got my beady eye on them, just in case they stray and become lost. Keeping tabs on them is difficult, though, especially if we're in a busy shopping centre or a theme park. But dressing them in matching outfits, particularly when we're on holiday, can help matters. Venezuela wears her own things now, but I often put the others in similarly coloured clothes so they're easier to spot from a distance

In Alder Hey hospital with Athena after her traumatic arrival in August 2021

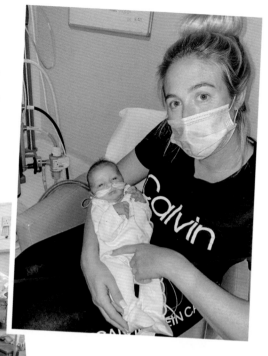

Athena's beautiful Christening with Valencia in July 2022

Me, aged 2

Above, with my sisters,
Romain and Montana,
and left, with Tyson

Above, at the beauty salon,
and left, with Mam and Dad

I love expecting a baby . . .

. . . and here I am learning the ropes with Venezuela

A typical Fury family day

Three in a bath

Nappy cream everywhere

Tyson with the double buggy and (from left to right) Adonis, Valencia, Prince, Tyson and Venezuela

Getting to school is the craziest time of day

Then it's free time in our outdoor play area

Me and Tyson with Prince, Valencia, Venezuela and little Tyson

We Furys love our food . . .

. . . whether it's a family meal
or home-made cake

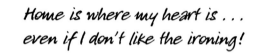

Home is where my heart is . . .
even if I don't like the ironing!

and can be distinguished from other kids. So the boys might all wear red tops and the girls might wear yellow tops, and I'll keep that in mind when we're out and about. This also makes shopping for outfits more straightforward. With so many children to dress, I just don't have the time to select individual things for them all.

Anyone walking past me in the street must think I've lost my mind, though, because I'm constantly counting out loud to double-check my kids are all present and correct. I'm sure all parents will recognise that heart-stopping feeling of panic when you suddenly lose sight of your child.

'One, two, three, four, five . . . *OH MY GOD, WHERE'S ADONIS – phew, there he is, hiding behind a lamp-post –* and six . . .'

But, in my experience, that protective instinct is emotional as well as practical. A large part of motherhood is being there for your children when they need you most, whether it's a cuddle if they're feeling sad or lonely, a heart-to-heart if they're having friendship troubles, or a pep talk if they're struggling with their confidence. I still rely on my own mam for love, support and guidance and I hope my kids will always feel they can rely on me, too.

Chapter Five

TABLE TALK

It won't come as any surprise to hear that feeding a big family like mine requires a huge amount of time, planning and preparation. Sometimes it can feel like a military operation. However, thanks to years of practice and a few handy hints and hacks, I've become quite good at managing the whole process.

Every week has its challenges. First, there's the supermarket big shop (*big* being the operative word) to ensure there's enough food to fill the cupboards and last us through. Next, there's the pressure of cooking hearty and nutritious meals that – all being well – everyone will eat and enjoy. Then I have to encourage six boisterous children to sit down at the kitchen table – plus Tyson, if he's at home – which is a feat in itself. So let's just say that teatime isn't an oasis of calm in the Fury household. In fact, some evenings it feels like feeding time at Blackpool Zoo, with dropped food, spilled drinks and deafening noise. I often find myself counting down the days until Saturday night, when – hooray! – I can order a family-sized takeaway and give myself a well-earned break.

Over the years I've acquired many kitchen tips from my relatives, none more so than my mam Lynda. She was a great cook when we were kids, rustling up delicious, traditional meat 'n' veg dishes like cottage pie, lamb hotpot and chicken casserole, the kind of tasty and filling meals the whole family could enjoy. She set such a great example.

* * *

Without exception, my week begins with the Monday supermarket shop. This usually takes place mid-morning, once the kids have been dropped off at school and nursery. I much prefer to do the 'big shop' alone these days, with just Athena in the trolley. In fact, having learned the hard way, I tend not to go anywhere near a supermarket if I have two or more children with me. When you've got a couple of them in tow, a shopping trip can become a total nightmare and take twice as long. When the little monkeys aren't having a major meltdown, they're either running amok and knocking down displays, or grabbing bags of sweets and cans of pop to sneak into the trolley. Shopping by myself, or just with Athena, means I can glide around the aisles at my own pace, without any of those aggravations or interruptions.

You might wonder why I don't make life easier still by shopping online and arranging a home delivery. I did try it a few years ago, when I was trying to avoid dragging Little Tyson, Valencia and Adonis to the supermarket. It didn't go particularly well. IT has never been my strong point, so it took me ages to find my way around the website and choose what I wanted. Then, when the goods were delivered the following morning, it turned out half of my order was out of stock. I ended up having to drive over to the supermarket to buy the missing items, which defeated the whole object. Ever since then, I've vowed to carry on shopping in the old-fashioned way. For me, it's the simplest and easiest option.

Occasionally, Tyson will accompany me because, with eight mouths to feed, I'm now at the stage where one trolley isn't enough to accommodate all the food we need. An extra pair of hands comes in useful, even if it does mean my husband being waylaid by a few selfie-hunting shoppers. You do see people doing a double-take when they spot their boxing hero in the local supermarket, shopping with his wife.

'Wow, didn't expect to see you two in here,' they'll say.

'Well, where d'you think we shop?' he'll reply with a smile.

If Tyson isn't around, I'll ask for assistance from one of the lovely staff members. They now come to expect me each Monday morning and, bless them, are usually on hand to help wheel my overloaded trolleys into the car park.

I've used the same Morecambe supermarket for over ten years (clue: it's the one with the green signage that begins with an 'A'). I know it like the back of my hand – I must have been hundreds of times – so am able to find everything I need quickly and easily. Tyson will sometimes suggest we try another store in town for a change, but when we do I just become totally disorientated – everything feels so unfamiliar – and I spend about twenty minutes longer than usual trying to locate the herbs and spices section. So I much prefer to stick to shopping in my tried and tested old faithful. I've never found the need to use the more expensive supermarkets, either. Why spend a fortune on a trolley-full of food, when you can get the same products cheaper elsewhere?

Like most savvy supermarket shoppers, I have a few tricks up my sleeve when it comes to buying goods. I'll always check for quality when I'm buying fresh produce – I can spot a bruised apple or a bendy carrot from a mile off – and, just like my mam used to do, I'll go rummaging at the back of shelves to find items with the longest 'use by' and 'best before' dates. I prefer to see and feel what I'm buying (which is another reason why I avoid online shopping). I'm constantly on the lookout for a good BOGOF or bulk-buy, and am not averse to the occasional yellow sticker bargain in the chiller cabinet if I know it's going to be eaten that same day.

I'm a creature of habit when I do the weekly shop; in fact, I virtually do it on autopilot. I try to buy enough stuff to cover five teatime meals, from Monday through to Friday. I don't write out a list – everything is stored in my head – and I'll already know ninety per cent of the items that are going to be thrown into the trolley; the remaining ten per cent accounts for impulse buys, or special offers that might take my fancy. I'll plan all the week's meals in advance, so I can head straight for the ingredients I need for a spaghetti Bolognese, for example, or a chicken and vegetable stew. I don't cook from scratch every evening (especially if I'm shuttling between the kids' dance classes or football practice) so two of those five meals might be twenty-minute bung-them-in-the-oven specials, like cheese and ham pizza or chicken nuggets and curly fries.

I'll also load up with various breakfast items, like porridge oats and crumpets, along with plenty of lunchtime sandwich options such as ham, cheese and tuna. I choose a nice selection of fresh fruit and vegetables, too, although the children much prefer the former over the latter (I'm sure mine aren't the only kids who need to be told repeatedly to eat their greens). Dairy products are a must – we go through vats of milk and stacks of yoghurts – and I'll always chuck in some freezer essentials, too, like Yorkshire puddings and oven chips.

My store-cupboard essentials include packets of rice and pasta (fusilli is my favourite), plus tins of baked beans and spaghetti, boxes of stock cubes and gravy granules, and an array of herbs, spices and sauces. I'm more than happy to buy cheaper own-brand products, although there are some famous names that I habitually stick to, like Heinz tomato ketchup, Hellman's mayonnaise and Nescafé instant coffee. The originals are often the best.

Meat and poultry probably takes up a good third of my supermarket shop – the Furys are all carnivores – but occasionally (and often before Easter and Christmas) I'll place a big order at a local butcher who offers home delivery. Buying meat in large quantities makes life a lot easier for me. I bag everything up into convenient portions and pack them into the freezer, to be defrosted when needed. The quality of this produce is fabulous, too – it's all locally reared – and because I'm buying in bulk it can work out to be very cost-effective. We may be more than comfortable, money-wise, but that doesn't mean I don't like a good deal when I see one. By spending wisely and sensibly, I also hope I'm setting a good example to the children, because I think it's really important they learn good habits for the future.

And finally, perched atop the trolley to avoid being crushed, come plenty of snacks and treats for six hungry children. This huge haul usually comprises three or four family-sized bags of assorted crisps, as well as a wide variety of 'boring' plain biscuits in packets (rich tea, custard creams and malted milk) and 'posh' chocolate biscuits in wrappers (KitKats, Blue Ribands and Breakaways). More often than not, this mountain of snacks is scoffed in the space of three days. 'When they're gone, they're gone,' I'll tell my kids but, despite this, they'll polish off the lot, like a plague of locusts. Any requests to replenish the snack-stash will always fall on deaf ears.

* * *

I'll level with you: I'm not a natural in the kitchen; never have been, never will be. If I'm able to make a nutritious meal that tastes good, fills up the family and doesn't give them food poisoning, that's a job well done in my book.

I know a lot of people love the whole process of cooking, and like experimenting with exotic flavours and recipes, but I just don't have that passion for it. I'm not saying I'm a bad cook – I do straightforward dishes quite well – but I don't think I'd give Delia or Nigella a run for their money. The family seem to like what I cook, though, and that's all that really matters to me.

My one and only attempt at being adventurous with food, when Tyson and I were newly-weds, ended pretty badly. In a bid to impress him, I decided to try a chicken and herb risotto that I'd spotted in a magazine. I paid over twenty pounds for the ingredients and spent most of the evening putting it together, only for it to come out of the pan smelling like bad feet. It didn't taste much better, either, and we could only manage a single forkful. It was a lesson learned. *Know your limitations, Paris. Stick to the simple stuff.*

When it comes to organising mealtimes in my current household, there have to be some rules in place. Firstly, every evening at 6 p.m., when Tyson's back from the gym, I insist we all sit round our kitchen table to eat. Not only is it easier for me to have everybody in one place, it also gives us half an hour to chat about our day, if we can get a word in edgeways. It may sometimes be total chaos, with kids shouting and cutlery flying, but for us it's important just to have that time together as a family.

My second mealtime rule is that we all eat the same dinner. In my kitchen, you get what you're given. Like many busy mothers, I have neither the time nor inclination to faff about making separate dishes, and I don't want to fall into the trap of making six different meals for six different kids. I realise they have their own likes and dislikes – I'll never please them all – so, to cater for everyone, I always ensure there's a lot of variety on the plate. A casserole is a good option, for instance, since I can shove in a good mix of meat, potatoes and other vegetables. One child might leave the meat, and another child might leave the potatoes, but at least they're all eating something.

So here's how the Fury family's midweek menu shapes up. Breakfast is the quickest (and craziest) meal of the day, since it usually involves the kids careering around the kitchen at eight o'clock, helping themselves to the contents of the fridge or the cupboards. It's vital they head off to school with their tummies full – I'm a great believer that breakfast is the most important meal of the day to set you up – so I make sure there's a decent supply of toast, cereal, fruit and yoghurt. I'll be on hand to help them with any hot breakfasts like porridge or Ready Brek and, if one of the kids is running late, I'll quickly make them a round of toast and jam to munch in the car.

As for lunchtimes, Prince, Little Tyson and Valencia all have school dinners. They all tell me they'd prefer to have packed lunches – I think they imagine a box full of snacks and junk food – but it's just not practical for me. It's hard enough scraping together a packed lunch for Adonis during the early-morning scramble (his nursery doesn't do hot meals), so doing four would be a bridge too far.

During school holidays, when everyone's at home, I'll make me and the kids simple lunches like cheese and ham toasties or pasta with tuna sauce. Years ago, when I had more time and fewer kids, I sometimes used to create those fancy, fiddly child-friendly lunches endorsed by parenting experts. I'd spend ages cutting out animal-shaped sandwiches, assembling clown-face pizzas and arranging fruit into sunshine shapes. These days, I'm afraid I just don't have the time. It's more of a case of grabbing what's available, whether that's a sausage roll or a yoghurt tube. The kids are perfectly happy with that.

Our evening meal merits a bit more preparation. I tend to stick to a small selection of simple, no-frills options that I'll cook in rotation. I often make enough food to cater for a dozen people: the eight of us, plus any extra guests. We often have unexpected drop-ins – from the kids' school friends to Tyson's boxing pals – so I'm always very well-prepared. If those additional meals aren't needed, I'll bag them up and pop them in the fridge for the next day's lunch. I sometimes do this with leftovers, too. Waste not, want not . . .

I prefer making traditional meat 'n' veg British dishes that appeal to the masses, like beef stew, cottage pie and boiled ham with cabbage and mash. I do a decent steak, too, with a creamy Diane sauce and chunky chips, and my roast dinners (lamb, chicken or beef, with potatoes and Aunt Bessie's Yorkshire puds) aren't half bad either. Occasionally I'll try something a little more exciting – I can just about stretch to chicken fajitas or spaghetti Bolognese – but anything more fancy will have the kids turning up their noses. A couple of them are very fussy eaters – Venezuela in particular – so I tend to avoid anything hot and spicy.

When time is tight, I will happily take the quick option, delving into the freezer compartment for pizzas, burgers or nuggets that can be ready in half an hour. Microwave meals don't really work for me because there's so many of us – it would take just as long to 'ping' eight dinners as it would to do something on the hob – but the occasional 'junk' meal doesn't hurt; most mams I know have some time-saving convenience food in reserve, and it's certainly not something I feel guilty about.

I've recently become a huge fan of the slow cooker – I use it once or twice a week now – although this method does need a bit more forward planning. In the morning, usually after the school run, I'll throw in all the ingredients, leave everything to bubble away for a few hours and – hey presto! – end up with a delicious, ready-to-serve meal. It's perfect for stews and casseroles (the slow-cooked meat comes out *so* tender it almost melts in the mouth) and I use it for a variety of soups, too, including my mam's favourite Scotch broth. I only wish I'd started using it years ago, because I can't believe how much time and effort it saves me. It's by far my favourite kitchen gadget and is pretty much foolproof, even for a simple cook like me.

Tyson rarely helps me out at mealtimes, but I'm not too bothered about that. I know there are plenty of men who are more than capable in the kitchen, and can take over the reins if needed, but my husband isn't one of them. This became very apparent a couple of years ago when, on a whim, he decided to cook the evening meal.

'Put your feet up, Paris,' he said. 'I'm going to make us all a proper, old-fashioned dinner.'

'Like what?' I asked, my heart sinking because I already knew how useless he was in the kitchen. In the early days of our marriage, Tyson had attempted a dish called 'Chicken à l'Orange' – a fried fillet smeared in mayo and ketchup – which was virtually inedible.

So Tyson came back from the butcher's with a carrier bag full of assorted offal: hearts, kidneys and livers, and

other organs I couldn't even identify. He emptied them
into a saucepan, covered them in water, shook over some
Bisto gravy granules and left them to simmer. After
about five hours, with the whole house smelling like
rotten dog food, he called us all into the kitchen and
started dishing out bowlfuls of lumpy grey sludge. It
looked absolutely disgusting. Unsurprisingly, none of us
would go near it – even Tyson decided to give it a miss
– and five minutes later the whole lot went to the neigh-
bour's dog. Other than manning the summer barbecue
(which, like with many men, appeals to his hunter-gath-
erer nature) my husband is now banned from any cooking duties. It's just not worth the hassle.

One of Tyson's favourite meals is a traditional
London Traveller dish known as bacon pudding (his
late grandmother was a southerner, and would make it
for him when he was a kid). During the coronavirus
lockdown, he developed a massive craving for it and,
as I had some time on my hands, I set about finding an
authentic recipe. I eventually got it off my Aunt
Romain, but there are many versions online if you
fancy trying it yourself! It's a bit of a faff to put together,
but I think it's worth it.

First of all, I make a dough with some plain flour and
suet, and roll it out into a large, flat rectangle. Then, I
cover it with a layer of lean bacon, chopped onion and

sliced tomatoes – it looks like a giant pizza – before rolling it up tightly like a jam roly-poly. Finally, I wrap it in a muslin cloth, secure it with some string and simmer it for three hours in a large pan of boiling water. I end up with a big, steaming dumpling, which tastes absolutely delicious sliced up and served with a dollop of mashed potato or a side of leafy green vegetables.

Tyson really loved sampling bacon pudding again – it brought back all his boyhood memories – although it has to be off the menu if he's training for a fight. Whenever that's the case, Tyson has to follow a very strict low-carb, protein-rich diet devised specially by his nutritionist. Gone are the days when, as part of the #TeamFury entourage, it was my job to keep him well fed and nourished before a big fight. He's won many a title belt on my grilled salmon and roast vegetables.

* * *

I try not to spend too much time in the kitchen at weekends. I prefer to take a break from cooking big meals, if I can, since I do my fair share between Monday and Friday. Most Saturday evenings, Tyson orders a bumper takeaway, normally from our local Chinese because we love the food there and all have our favourite dishes. When it arrives, I'll load up with my usual sweet and sour chicken, shredded beef and egg fried rice, alongside nibbles like spare ribs and prawn crackers. It's so nice to be able to just close the kitchen door and put my feet up, while enjoying scrumptious food that someone else has cooked.

Years ago I used to cook a roast dinner every weekend, and I still do occasionally, but as our family has expanded we're now much more likely to go out for our Sunday lunch. Not only is it far less hassle for me, it's nice for us all to have a change of scenery and to spend some quality time together. We tend to stick to a handful of child-friendly places in the Morecambe and Lancaster area where the staff know our family well, and where we're treated like any other diners. The locals are used to seeing us out and about, so it's no big deal when the Furys arrive for their Sunday roast.

Tyson and I rarely choose anything else off the pub grub menu – we're creatures of habit, and we love a good carvery – and the children will either opt for the same as us, or choose one of the special kids' meals. Our brood are also told to behave nicely and watch their table manners, of course, but, you can almost guarantee that at least one of them will kick off at some point, whingeing because they're not allowed to run amok in the pub, or crying because their sister's ice cream sundae is bigger than theirs. But that's the beauty of going to a family pub, as opposed to a posh restaurant, because other parents with kids will be in the exact same boat. You don't feel so guilty if your toddler has a meltdown, because the same thing might be happening on the next-door table, too!

Our eating regime is definitely more relaxed at the weekend. On Saturday and Sunday mornings we'll have what we call our 'family breakfast', which, compared with the midweek madness, is a far more leisurely affair. I'll serve up simple snacks like scrambled eggs or beans on toast, or perhaps waffles or pancakes. If Tyson isn't on a strict, pre-fight diet, and fancies a full English breakfast, he'll invariably head over to his favourite café in Morecambe. His OCD goes into overdrive if I do a fry-up at home – it being such a multitasking meal, I always make a mess – so I understand where he's coming from. In any case, I'm not a fan of a big cooked breakfast; I find it far too heavy and much prefer a lighter bite in the morning.

The kids will have beakers or bottles of water with their breakfast, since they tend to prefer that over milk and fruit juices (I'm not complaining, and it keeps the dentist happy that they're not always having sweet drinks), while Tyson and I are big coffee drinkers, although we're at different ends of the coffee spectrum. I'm quite content with Nescafé instant granules – fully caffeinated; I need that pep-up – and like it made very weak with lots of milk, but no sugar. If I'm having a hot drink in town, I'll choose a latte or a flat white; nothing too strong or bitter for me.

Tyson, on the other hand, has become a coffee connoisseur (or a 'coffee snob' as I call him). His obsession began when he was holed up in a US training camp that happened to have an all-singing, all-dancing coffee machine. A freshly made Americano – with hot steamed milk – soon became his daily treat, something for him to really look forward to. Then, perhaps to break the monotony of camp life, he began to educate himself on the origins of the beans – Kenya, Brazil, Colombia – as well their various blends and roasts.

When he returned to the UK, Tyson splashed out on his own top-of-the-range coffee machine. It's his pride and joy (he loves it as much as his Ferrari, I reckon) and it's kept permanently in his camp HQ in Morecambe so the kids can't tamper with it. Once or twice a day he'll grind his own beans and, with tender loving care, will make himself his perfect brew. His coffee fetish has become a standing joke between us, in fact. He'll ridicule my mugs of cheap Nescafé, and I'll poke fun at his posh Americanos.

'Not such a working-class man of the people now, eh, Tyson?'

'Oh, go and boil your kettle . . .'

He knows I'm only winding him up. Considering what we've been through in the past, I'll choose a coffee addiction over an alcohol addiction any day of the week.

Tyson and I are on the same page when it comes to having wine, beer and spirits in the house. We avoid it, if at all possible. His problems with alcohol abuse have been well documented, and neither of us want to go back to that awful time. In the depths of his depression my husband regularly drank himself into a stupor, and I'd have to go roaming the bars, pubs and alleyways of Morecambe to drag him back home. I was thankful for small mercies, though, because – even at his worst – he did most of his binge-drinking out of the house, away from the gaze of the children. Those dark days are long gone, thank goodness, and while Tyson will enjoy the occasional drink – especially after a fight, when that ice-cold beer is well deserved – he's able to control his intake. He knows when to stop, and when not to overdo it.

These days, we don't keep much alcohol in the house at all. If you look in our cupboards you're more likely to see a bottle of Ribena than a bottle of red wine. We only really get the drinks in at Christmas or if we're hosting a summer-time garden barbecue. Whenever we receive a gift like a magnum of champagne or some fancy

Scotch whisky, we won't dream of cracking it open immediately. Instead, we'll keep it stored away until our friends and family come over, at which point we'll bring it out to share with our guests. It's a nice, sociable thing to do. On the whole, it's very rare for Tyson and me to enjoy a drink at home. We're far more likely to curl up on the sofa with a glass of cordial or a cup of coffee. I know it may sound boring, but that's the way we like it. We both know from experience that there are much worse alternatives.

* * *

Encouraging your children to eat healthily is one of the trickier elements of parenting. It's a tough nut to crack. I do my best to guide my kids in the right direction but it can often feel like an uphill struggle, whether it's curbing their snacking or dealing with their likes and dislikes. At evening mealtimes, I aim to provide them with a varied and balanced diet, which usually means lots of protein, like meat and poultry, served alongside carbohydrates (potatoes, rice or pasta) and a selection of vegetables. For 'afters', I always have a big bowlful of fruit on the kitchen table – they're all big fruit eaters, thank goodness – and, as an alternative, I make sure there are plenty of yoghurts in the fridge.

I'd prefer my children not to eat in between meals, if I'm honest – they shouldn't need to if they're eating enough at breakfast, lunch and tea – but, to satisfy any hunger pangs (especially when they come back from school), I stock up with a few snacks and nibbles. Depriving them of goodies isn't necessarily a good idea, in my opinion – they'd only crave them and buy them elsewhere – but I do try to exert a bit of control. I might, for example, ask them to limit their snacking to one bag of crisps and two biscuits per day; but I'm afraid they don't always listen and often eat me out of house and home. So the big rule is that I won't replace them once they're gone. I'm quite firm in that regard.

My only other rule is that I don't allow any snacking after 5 p.m. Firstly, I don't want them to ruin their tea and, secondly, I don't want any sugar rushes keeping them awake at night. And while I don't let the kids take hot meals away from the table and into other rooms (primarily to prevent smears and spills on my nice sofas and carpets), I'm not super-strict about snacks. At the weekends, I don't mind them taking crisps and popcorn into the lounge to watch TV, or up to their bedroom to watch a movie. I'm not so house-proud that I feel the need to follow them around with a dustpan and brush.

I rarely buy them sweets and chocolate, however – I try my best to protect their teeth – but with Tyson being much more indulgent, it can be very frustrating. It makes a mockery of my healthy eating message and can create friction between the two of us.

'I don't know why I bother . . .' I'll huff. 'Don't blame me if they get a mouthful of fillings.'

'Ah, it's just a treat,' he'll smile. 'I'll make sure they clean their teeth afterwards, don't you worry . . .'

I'm also quite hardline about fizzy pop. We never have it in the house other than as a treat at Christmas, because if we did, it'd get guzzled in days. Instead, I buy bottles of sugar-free cordial and encourage the children to drink lots of water.

To a certain extent, I also feel obliged to keep a close eye on the amount my kids consume, as well as what they consume. It's a really fine line to tread. I might have a quiet word with the older ones if I think they're overeating (or undereating) but I'll always do this in a sensitive manner. I certainly wouldn't want to trigger any food aversions or body image issues. If I notice anything is amiss – maybe I'll find far too many crisp bags in their coat pocket – I'll have a quiet word, perhaps suggesting they go easy on the snacks. Good health comes from within, I'll tell them, and is linked to all the vitamins and nutrients they get from a balanced diet. And eating sensibly doesn't just help them maintain a healthy weight; it also benefits their skin, their hair, even their concentration levels.

How much they take on board, who knows, but I can only do my best. While I want them to have a positive relationship with food – and to maintain a healthy appetite – I also want them to recognise when their eating habits have veered off course. If my children were to suffer any diet-related issues or illnesses in their adult life, I'd hate for them to turn round and say, 'Mam, why did you never mention anything when we were younger?' I think it's a parent's responsibility to keep tabs on their kids in this manner, so that any issues can be addressed sooner rather than later.

* * *

From the eldest down to the youngest, all of my kids have gone through stages of fussy eating. Venezuela, for example, has been very picky since she was a toddler; she still has really bland tastes, and tends to opt for anything beige-coloured (if I didn't encourage her to eat more fruit and veg, she'd happily live on bread, cereal and biscuits).

At the other end of the age scale, Athena – the baby of the family – coped really well with the weaning process, but now and again will refuse her evening meal. The progression from infant food to grown-up meals can be a challenging phase for many parents, but I've always tried to keep things simple. When the time was right for Athena to progress from baby rice to solid food, I began to spoon-feed her mashed up versions of our own family meals. I ensured these little bowlfuls didn't contain extra salt, or any other strong flavours, and would add a little water or milk to obtain the desired consistency; not too lumpy, not too runny.

Dishes like chicken stew and cottage pie went down a treat with Athena – as did rice pudding for dessert – and she soon became familiar with the taste of my cooking. On the odd occasion she spat something out – she wasn't a fan of steamed vegetables – I had a few jars of shop-bought baby food on standby. I prefer not to use them, if I can help it, but needs must with a hungry child.

Encouraging a fidgety baby or toddler to finish their dinner, without it ending up in their hair, down the high-chair or on the floor, can really test your patience and tolerance. After sitting there for half an hour, you'll try all sort of daft games to persuade them to eat. Last year, around Christmas-time, Athena refused point blank to try some mash and gravy and I had to resort to desperate measures. I decided to film her on my phone, just to demonstrate the lengths to which parents have to go.

'Shall we feed the little Christmas elf?' I asked, while dangling her favourite festive decoration in front of her nose. I pretended to give Santa's little helper a mouthful of food, before repeating this with Athena. Much to my relief, this 'spoonful for him . . . spoonful for you' tactic worked a treat, and the bowl was soon empty.

I uploaded the clip onto Instagram, asking my followers, 'So what games and tricks do *you* know?' and was deluged with responses from frazzled mams and dads with similar problems and solutions. As a parent, sometimes it's good to know you're not alone. Behind the scenes, we're all fighting our own battles!

My eldest son Prince probably has the heartiest appetite of all. Ironically enough, though, he's the only one who has to avoid certain ingredients due to being diagnosed with a food allergy. When he was aged about five, we started to notice his face swelling up following mealtimes – his eyes would close up, and his lips would tingle – and we couldn't figure out what was triggering it. It came as quite a shock when hospital tests revealed that Prince had an allergy to shellfish. The doctors told him to avoid any food containing things like prawns, shrimps and mussels, and to carry a supply of antihistamines with him at all times.

Having a child with an allergy can be quite worrying for a parent, but I'm reassured by the fact that Prince is extremely careful about what he eats, especially when he's out and about, and will always double-check the ingredients on menus and packets (as will I, if I'm with him). Fortunately, restaurants and other eateries have to be very clued up about food allergies and intolerances nowadays. Most places can cater for him quite easily.

Whether they have allergies or not, I think it's useful for children to take an interest in the food they eat. I hope my kids realise that their meals don't suddenly appear on the plate as if by magic, but require thought and preparation. Now that Venezuela's getting older I've been trying to teach her some cookery basics, just like Mam did with me, but I can't say it's filled her with enthusiasm. Like many teenagers, she probably has better things to do with her time than peeling vegetables, chopping meat and perfecting gravy. I'm persevering, though – she knows she can't rely on ready meals if she has her own family – and I'll do exactly the same with the other kids, too. Passing on these life skills is important, I think.

Baking cakes, however, is less of a hard sell to my children. Like many bored-as-heck Brits, the Fury family became obsessed with baking during the coronavirus lockdown, and you could barely move in our kitchen for biscuits, muffins and puddings. The kids loved getting involved in the whole process – the weighing, the sifting, the stirring – and liked discovering how basic ingredients like eggs, flour, sugar and butter could create such delicious little cakes. Little Tyson particularly enjoyed helping me in the kitchen, and we were very proud of our raspberry pavlova and banoffee pie. He often says he wants to become a chef when he's older. I'd love that. I don't mind what my kids do, career-wise, as long as they're happy.

Sadly – but unsurprisingly – when lockdown ended I got out of the baking habit. These days I hardly have any spare time on my hands and, for reasons of convenience, most of our baked goods come straight off the supermarket shelves. We don't tend to bother with big desserts during the week, in any case – we'll generally grab a yoghurt or a piece of fruit – but at weekends I'll sometimes buy a jumbo apple pie or a couple of strawberry cheesecakes. Maybe I should make the effort to put on my apron again, and plug in the food mixer. I still treasure those memories of baking carrot cake and banana bread on a lazy Sunday afternoon. Quality time with the kids, plus a warm slice of cake afterwards . . . what could be better?

Encouraging my children to eat healthily can be a battle – I think everyone would agree it's one of the trickiest parts of parenting – but I can only do my best. So I'm trying to be a good role model to them, encouraging a balanced diet and home-cooked meals, but also helping them to see food as one of life's pleasures, especially when it's shared and enjoyed together round the family dinner table.

Chapter Six

NO PLACE LIKE HOME . . .

As someone who spends a lot of time at home, keeping the family space in good order is very important to me. I want my house to be somewhere that's not only safe and clutter-free (particularly when small children are hurtling around) but is also warm and welcoming, the sort of place where our guests can sit back and relax. Tyson and I have lived in a handful of places throughout our marriage – they've got progressively larger with each move – but we've led a relatively settled life. Although my husband and I were both raised in trailers, we spent our entire childhood in the same places – me in Doncaster, him in Manchester – before beginning our married life in a caravan close to Lancaster. When Venezuela and Prince were young we bought a two-bedroomed bungalow in nearby Morecambe (we'd grown fond of the resort, having visited it at weekends) and, when the family grew bigger, we upsized to a detached property by the coast.

More recently, we've been lucky enough to move into our dream home, a beautiful manor-style house on the outskirts of the town. Both Tyson and I realised it was time to relocate. We definitely needed more space – our five (soon to be six) children had outgrown our house by the sea – and we also needed more privacy. Tyson's celebrity status had started to attract bystanders and rubberneckers; some would linger outside the house for hours, trying to catch a glimpse of him, and others would knock on our door and roam around our garden. It became pretty scary at times. So, for the sake of our family's safety and security, we decided to up sticks and make the move.

As soon as Tyson and I viewed the manor house, we knew it was the one for us. Its semi-rural location was ideal – just a short drive from town, and a quick stroll to the countryside – and, being surrounded by trees and fences, it felt reassuringly secluded. The design and layout of the house really suited us, too, as there was plenty of space and storage (among the first things I look for, as someone who can't stand clutter). Being quite a modern property, it didn't need much renovation, either, which was a definite plus point. Since moving in, we've hardly had to make any structural alterations, just a few cosmetic changes here and there to put our own stamp on the place.

Our new place is big, but it still has a very homely feel. That's really important to me. I like my house to have a warm, welcoming and 'lived-in' vibe, somewhere that feels totally relaxed and comfortable. I've never desired a 'look-but-don't-touch' show home; instead, I want friends and family (and their kids) to be able to lounge on the couch, put their feet up and feel at home, rather than worrying about crumbs on carpets or fingerprints on walls. I've got one house rule for visitors – shoes off at the door! – but, other than that, people can rest assured that the Fury place is a chill-out zone.

First-time visitors usually ask for a quick tour around. I usually start off in the room I spend the most time in: the kitchen diner. This is our family hub, the real heart of the household, where we all congregate to eat, drink and chat. Big and square, with a cream marble floor and burgundy marble worktops, it has a long, fourteen-seater table on one side, and a large range cooker on the other. The lovely French windows open out onto the garden play area, handily enough, which means I can keep an eye on the kids while I make tea; I like to have them in my vision, especially the little ones.

Another door leads into a good-sized utility room, where I store my washer and my dryer, as well as various mops, brushes and an array of cleaning fluids. As someone who devotes much of her life to house-work, an engine room like this is an absolute must-have for me.

The front door leads into a light and airy hallway, part of which is cordoned off to make a play area for the youngsters. It's a really useful space that houses their big and bulky toys, from Disney castles to mini-kitchens, and the kids and their pals really love spending time there. Either side of the hallway, we have two very roomy living areas. Our family lounge contains a super-sized twelve-seater horseshoe-shaped sofa, and a big coffee table, both of which are angled towards a wall-mounted 72-inch television. It's an ideal room for watching movies and playing board games, as well as for admiring Tyson's trophies, belts and framed photographs, which are all proudly on display. Entering this room, with all its amaz-ing memorabilia, can be quite an eye-opening experience for anyone visiting for the first time.

In contrast, the 'fancy' living room is a more formal lounge for the grown-ups. This is the only area of the house that's strictly off-limits to the children, especially the young ones with their runny noses and sticky fingers. It's a very ornate room, decorated in a classical style with a royal blue and gold colour scheme. There are three velvet couches arranged around a rectangular coffee table, with its pile of glossy lifestyle books. My wedding gifts and family heirlooms, like the Royal Crown Derby crockery and the Waterford crystalware, are all on display in this room, too. I don't spend as much time in here as I'd like, sadly – I'm just too busy with the kids – but I do sometimes daydream about sitting alone on my blue sofa, maybe when the children are older and less demanding, sipping a coffee and reading my posh coffee-table books about fancy holidays and faraway places that Tyson and I might visit.

Across the hallway, on the same side as the family lounge, we have our dining room, a lovely, large space that contains a beautiful twenty-foot, sixteen-seater marble table that we had shipped over from Italy. At either end we have golden thrones with red velvet cushions, Tyson's tongue-in-cheek nod to his 'Gypsy King' status. We don't have much over-the-top furniture in our house, but I allowed my husband this one-off extravagance. We only tend to dine in this room on special occasions, like Easter Sunday or Christmas Day; most of our family meals are eaten in our kitchen, which is much more childproof. Take it from me, it's much easier to wipe gravy and ketchup off floor tiles than a thick-pile carpet.

More recently, Tyson and I have started to use the dining room as our work space. In the evenings, when the kids are in bed, we'll shut the door, pull up a seat (or throne!) at the table and answer our emails or attend to our paperwork. It's our preferred location for Zoom meetings or media interviews, too, so if you ever see either of us on *BBC Breakfast* or *This Morning*, we're beaming to you live from the dining room . . .

A solid oak staircase leads to the first floor, where the family bedrooms are located. Ours is a pretty big space; it's more like a suite, with a three-seater sofa and a huge emperor bed (we needed one big enough to fit the four younger kids, who often snuggle up with us for movie 'n' popcorn nights). Little Athena's cot is beside our bed, so I can keep a close eye on her. We'll move her out when we think she's old enough to sleep in her own bed, perhaps around her second birthday. Most of our babies have stayed in our room for a couple of years, at the very least; any younger just doesn't feel right to me. Other parents may disagree but, as I always say, 'each to their own'.

Venezuela's pink bedroom is across the landing – complete with her own make-up station – as is Prince's room, painted in blue, which has a PlayStation, an Xbox and a comfy gaming chair. The three middle children – Little Tyson, Valencia and Adonis – all share the same large room, each with their own single bed. Their walls are painted in a colourful fairy-tale theme, depicting knights, princesses, castles and palaces. We asked a professional artist to create this specially for us, and she did a really fantastic job. I have a feeling we'll have to update it to pop stars and superheroes when the kids get older.

The top floor of our house comprises two guest bedrooms with ensuite bathrooms. Both are in a permanent state of readiness, with fluffy towels and fresh bedlinen, since we tend to have lots of visitors. Every other weekend we'll usually have friends or relatives stopping over; my mam and dad, perhaps, or my brother-in-law Shane. House guests are always welcomed with open arms – even if they turn up out of the blue. There'll always be a room and a meal ready for them. I love it when the house is buzzing with people. The more the merrier.

Last but not least, on the first floor I have my very own dressing room. I know it's a bit of a luxury, but I've dreamed of having one for ages. I've always loved clothes – check out my Insta feed if you need further proof! – and have accumulated many items over the years, bought from high street stores and haute couture designers. So my special room comprises plenty of deep drawers and floor-to-ceiling wardrobes for my clothes, whether that's regular leisure wear or glamorous evening wear. Everything is colour-coded, so I can pick and choose with ease. I also asked the builders to install a light-up display unit for my shoe and handbag collection; I've a real soft spot for chic leather goods. There is also a home here for a selection of sentimental outfits belonging to family members, like christening gowns, birthday costumes and then the designer dresses I've worn for title fights. Hung up on one of the rails is my favourite ever item of clothing, a black Moschino jacket (with sparkly embellished dollar signs) that I wore for Tyson's fight against Wladimir Klitschko in 2015.

While I love my clothes, I also have regular wardrobe clearouts. If I find an item that I no longer like, or that has served its purpose for me, I'll donate it to friends, family or charity. I reckon there must be dozens of Morecambe residents walking around in Paris Fury's designer gear! I do the same with household items, too. When a gadget has hardly been used – like the electric blender that sat on my worktop for months, doing nothing – I'll eventually get rid or recycle. But, when I'm loading a bag full of old toys and games, I have to double-check that the kids aren't massively attached to anything, no matter how well-used it is. I don't think my life would be worth living if I took Adonis' precious Spider-Man figure to the charity shop . . .

* * *

I wouldn't say I'm an expert in interior design, or have a particular flair for it. Neither do I have the time or inclination to flick through issues of *Homes & Gardens* or watch *DIY SOS* on TV. But I know what I like, and I know what best suits my living space. I'd describe my style as classical, but comfortable: think Olde English country manor, with lots of neutral colours and natural materials. Luckily, Tyson and I share exactly the same taste in interiors – neither of us likes the modern or minimalistic look – and we do wonder where our influences and inspirations have come from. We were both raised in modest trailers, by parents who had little interest in interior design other than keeping everything shipshape. I do share my mam's fondness for precious silverware and glassware, however; she had a beautiful collection of both and, when I was a child, I'd help her to clean and polish them.

I don't like anything too way-out or wacky and feel no need to make a statement or follow a trend. When I'm choosing flooring and wall coverings, my base colours are invariably white, cream and beige; boring, I know, but I've always opted for neutral palettes and plain surfaces. I couldn't live with vivid colours and vibrant designs – facing them every day would give me a headache – and I'd also be worried that they'd date very quickly. At least with a blank canvas you're never likely to go out of fashion. And you can add colour and interest in other ways, by pepping up a beige sofa with some bright cushions, for instance, or jazzing up a plain wall with a vibrant painting.

Then, if you fancy a change, you can swap these pieces around, or even replace them with new items. And you don't need to spend a fortune on these little extras; I often visit high street stores (even pound shops) to buy accessories like candles and cushions. To be honest, I think many expensive versions are a total rip-off; the cheap and cheerful alternatives are often just as good. Why waste your money when there's hardly any difference in quality? Even when it comes to furniture, Tyson and I will happily mix and match designer pieces from Italy with less pricey items from Dunelm.

I'm not very hands-on when it comes to painting and decorating. Neither is Tyson. Because it's not our forte, and since we don't want to make a pig's ear of it, we usually draft in experts to do a proper job. I often ask tradespeople to leave spare pots of gloss and emulsion, though, so I can touch up the paintwork if necessary. When you have young children, you become used to finding ink, crayon or fingerprints on the walls and windowsills. I've had a few disasters in my time. In our previous house, Little Tyson and his cousins once got hold of my make-up bag and decided to daub the staircase walls and carpets with my red Chanel lipstick. A few coats of paint sorted out the defaced wall area, but the carpet was a lost cause. And, worse still, I had to shell out for more lippy.

'You'll *never* have an immaculate home with a load of little kids,' Mam will say. 'That won't happen until they've flown the nest . . .'

Tyson and I are reasonably good at DIY, though, and can manage minor jobs like changing plugs or putting up shelves. We'll call in the professionals for any larger undertakings, such as wall-tiling or floor-laying. But when it comes to constructing things, like flat-pack furniture, I make a much better fist of it than Tyson. His patience levels are much lower than mine. He doesn't follow instructions very well and, because his hands are so huge, he's totally useless with tiny parts and screws. If we're assembling a kids' desk, for example, he'll get really frustrated with the fiddly bits and will storm off, leaving his more tolerant wife to get the job done perfectly.

My practical skills didn't quite extend to building our outdoor adventure play area. I've always loved the idea of our children having their own private little park so, just after we moved in, I asked a specialist company to design one for us. It features the usual playground attractions – swings, slides, climbing frames – and, because it's built on artificial grass, can be utilised in all weathers, any time of year. It's proved to be such a great investment. Our youngest four love it, as do their friends and cousins, and they often spend hours outside having fun. I don't like cooping my kids up indoors for too long – playing on their consoles for hours isn't healthy for mind or body – so this is a great way for them to get some fresh air and exercise.

We don't have a traditional garden; I'd describe it as more like a very large backyard. While Tyson would love a proper grassy lawn, surrounded by plants and shrubs, I've put him off the idea, because it's too high-maintenance. Neither of us are keen gardeners – we're not remotely interested in it – and to keep it looking nice we'd have to forever rely on help. Not only that, but with all the rainfall we get in the north-west of England a lawn would get wet and boggy, and I couldn't cope with the kids constantly tramping mud into the house. It would drive me crazy. So I've persuaded Tyson to opt for Tarmac instead, with a few planted-up containers and hanging baskets dotted about to add some colour.

With children and toddlers roaming around the place, be it in the yard or in the house, I'm always mindful of health and safety issues. Indoors, stairgates are a must-have and, to be extra-safe, I put a set at the top and at the bottom. I also have special child locks on the low-level kitchen cupboards, to stop them accessing any breakable items or cleaning products. I do my best to make our furniture as child-friendly as possible, too, so try to avoid buying tables with sharp corners or displaying fragile ornaments that could be easily knocked over (the most precious ones are kept safe in cabinets).

I do my best to teach the children about safety awareness and accident prevention, and will tell the younger ones to stay away from the cooker hob when it's on, for example, and to avoid climbing on tables or chests of drawers that may topple over. Venezuela and Prince aren't too old for advice, either, and I will often warn them not to use devices in the bathroom – water and electricity don't mix, of course – and to take care when using kitchen appliances like kettles and toasters.

I'm vigilant whenever we're away too. If I'm visiting friends and family with Athena and Adonis in tow – or if we're in a holiday home – I'll often do a quick recce of the place to spot any potential risks or hazards. That being said, most of my pals have their own kids as well, so their homes tend to be extremely child-friendly in any case. Like me, they wouldn't dream of putting glass vases or silver candlesticks within the reach of little ones. That would be a recipe for disaster.

It's impossible to totally baby-proof a house, though. Accidents are bound to happen with young children, whether it's trapping their fingers in a door (like Adonis did last Christmas, poor thing) or bumping their heads on a cupboard door that's been mistakenly left ajar. In the kitchen, I have a high-up cupboard that houses all my first aid supplies: the usual stuff like plasters, bandages and antiseptic cream for cuts and grazes, as well as medication such as Calpol (for high temperatures) and Piriton (for hay fever and allergies). I'm always careful to keep this cupboard well stocked, and regularly check for out-of-date medications that need to be disposed of. I consider it one of the more important household jobs; the last thing I want to do is ever put my children's health at risk.

* * *

I may not have a conventional nine-to-five job but, in my eyes, keeping my house and family in check is a full-time occupation in itself. In fact, I get quite irritated when people suggest that stay-at-home mothers 'don't work', as if we laze around the place all day, lying on a chaise longue and eating grapes. I can safely say that running a household while raising six children (often single-handedly, if Tyson is away) is no walk in the park. It can be ridiculously demanding, both physically and emotionally. In fact, my friends who go out to work often say it's far more stressful in the home than in the office. Some of them are quite happy for their local nursery or childminder to take the strain.

And, to anyone who assumes I have a housekeeper to assist with the domestic duties, let me set the record straight: I don't. Never have, never will. Even though I could quite easily afford a full-time cleaner, I choose to tackle the vast majority of chores myself, with a little help from Tyson and the kids.

There's only one household job I don't do, and that's the ironing. I hate it with a passion. I used to tackle it all myself but, when the fourth or fifth child came along, the mound of clothes grew into a mountain, and my ironing time went up to six hours per week. It became totally overwhelming. Because I was rushing through the pile, sometimes late into the night, I started to get a bit slapdash – Tyson would moan about the creases in his shirts – and before long I realised I really did need outside help with this job. Despite my best efforts I wasn't getting it done properly, and it was time to delegate it to someone who could.

Now, every Monday, I send bagfuls of freshly washed and dried clothes to a local lady who does it all brilliantly (no creased shirts, much to Tyson's relief) and brings it back in neatly folded piles, for me to transfer to drawers and wardrobes. She's an absolute godsend. I couldn't do without her now. I felt slightly guilty when I first started using her – I genuinely felt like I was cheating – but not any more. I do all the other household jobs, so I think I'm allowed this one time-saving luxury.

As for the rest of the housework, I wouldn't say I particularly enjoy doing it. To me, it's purely functional. Some people love the whole cleaning process – it's prompted a whole industry of books and TV shows, after all – but I just see it as a means to an end; something to be done as swiftly as possible so I can get on with the rest of my day. I'll never leave the house until all my jobs are done, though; only when the house is clean and fresh will I allow myself to go to the gym, do some shopping or, if he's around, grab an early-evening meal in town with Tyson. That's the moment when, if I ever need the children looking after, my babysitter Gabby will usually step in. It's such a blessing having her around.

So a typical day's housework will start for me at around 7.30 a.m. If I know I'm spending the morning cleaning,

I'll tie my hair up into a bun, or back into a neat ponytail, and put on a matching hoodie and tracksuit bottoms (I really hate looking scruffy, even when I'm shaking rugs and squeezing bleach down a toilet). Once the kids are up and about, I'll whizz into each bedroom to make their beds, if they've not done that already, and perhaps give their bathrooms a quick wipe-over.

I'll open the windows to give everywhere a good airing, and will check under the bed for any discarded socks or sweet wrappers. After the kids have been dropped off at school and nursery (usually by Tyson, if he's not training for a big fight) I'll have my breakfast, often with Athena by my side, and will then clear up the kitchen, wiping down worktops, emptying bins and loading the dishwasher.

Then it's time to make sure Venezuela's awake; unlike her younger brother Prince, she's pretty sprightly in the mornings and is usually dressed and ready to go by 9 a.m. She'll usually help me with chores until lunchtime, after which she'll have a couple of lessons with her home tutor, usually in the peaceful environment of the dining room. Venezuela is following the standard GCSE curriculum, studying subjects including maths, English, history and biology. She works extremely hard and Tyson and I are so pleased with the progress she's making. Our daughter is a great role model for the younger children – the perfect big sister! – and we're very proud of her.

After a big mug of coffee (I need that hit of caffeine in the morning!) I'll have a quick look around the house, to work out which jobs are more pressing. More often than not, my first task is to tackle the overflowing laundry bin. You can only imagine how much washing a family of eight generates. Once I've loaded the first batch of clothes into the machine – the whites, perhaps – I might vacuum upstairs and downstairs, while Venezuela gets on with another job, like polishing the mirrors or mopping the kitchen floor. Two or three times per week, we might jointly tackle a more time-intensive chore. That might be cleaning the windows top to bottom, or clearing out the bedroom drawers and wardrobes. Venezuela is such a great help, and never complains. She just gets on with things. We're quite similar in that respect.

So from 10 a.m. to 3 p.m., while the kids are at school, I can guarantee that my house will be clean and orderly. However, between hometime and bedtime, I have to forget about being house-proud for a few hours. As the children let off steam and drag out their toys, the place can look like a bomb site. And while the mess and the clutter makes me shudder – especially if I've been cleaning all day – I just have to shrug my shoulders

All packed and ready to go . . .

. . . for our fun
in the sun

We love our UK days out

Having fun
whatever the
weather!

Celebrating the good times

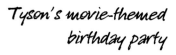

Valencia's 3rd birthday
and little Tyson's 4th

Athena's gender reveal – the pink
powder stained my floor tiles!

Montana's baby shower

Tyson's movie-themed
birthday party

Date nights and
romantic getaways

Backstage with Ed Sheeran

I'm always there for
Tyson's title fights

Getting away to Dubai and New York

Keeping fit –
essential for all the
energy I need

I always enjoy my
TV appearances,
whether it's at home
or in the studio

Getting ready for my girls' night out

With my friends

My wonderful mam

My beloved Granny Mary

I cherish every moment of planning and celebrating our family milestones

Athena's christening in July 2022

Preparing the party table

Adonis's special Spiderman-themed 3rd birthday in 2022

and let them get on with it. During this window of time I never bother tidying up after them, no matter how strong the impulse. I have to remind myself that the house belongs to the children, too, and they have every right to use it as a play space, so long as they're treating the house with respect and aren't completely wrecking the joint.

Once they're all tucked up in bed, however, I'll tour the house, checking each room and peering into every nook and cranny. Every game will be returned to the toy box, every book will be replaced on the shelf, and every crisp packet or drinks carton will be chucked in the bin. By the time the clock strikes eight, it's officially a Clutter-free Zone.

'Wow, you wouldn't even know we had six kids . . .' I'll say to Tyson as we relax on the couch, relishing a few hours of peace and quiet before the chaos resumes in the morning.

Having a large property means I get through dozens of bottles of cleaning products each month. I'm a big fan of good old-fashioned bleach, for keeping the kitchen and bathroom nice and germ-free, and I also use lots of Zoflora disinfectant for floors and surfaces. I couldn't do without my microfibre cloths, either, which I can use wet or dry (and with or without cleaning fluids) to pick up dust and dirt. I always pay a little more for good-quality cloths, because they tend to be more absorbent and long-lasting; sometimes you do get what you pay for. Other must-have products include my Mr Muscle window cleaner – I find it's one of the few sprays that doesn't streak my windows – and Fairy Liquid, which I use for stain removal on fabrics as well as washing the dishes.

'Act quickly!' is my best advice with regard to stains on clothes and furnishings. The faster you act the better, because the offending substance will have less time to sink in and become permanent. For liquid spillages, I always try to blot rather than scrub. I've had all sorts of stuff on my carpets over the years – Ribena, red wine, tomato sauce – and, whenever this happens, I'll immediately make a dash for some kitchen roll or an old tea towel. I'll then try to soak up as much of the stain as I can without scrubbing, even if that means applying countless sheets of paper until everything's absorbed. If that doesn't do the trick, I'll go for Plan B – the Fairy Liquid option – diluting it with some water and giving the carpet a good dab. And failing that ... well, I just have to live with an annoying pink stain or hide it beneath an item of furniture!

From removing stains to reducing waste, social media and YouTube are full of household hacks. Some friends of mine swear by vinegar or lemon juice to polish windows, or bicarbonate of soda to keep things fresh and odour-free, but I tend to stick to conventional cleaning fluids. The only top tip I've discovered for myself happened by accident. Tyson always has a pile of memorabilia to personally sign at home – his books, his photographs, his boxing gloves – so often walks around clutching a Sharpie pen. The black ink can get everywhere, especially on the kitchen table and the worktops, and, for a long while, I couldn't find any detergents that would remove it.

One day there happened to be a hairspray can in the kitchen (don't ask me why!), so I grabbed it on the off-chance and gave the stubborn Sharpie stain a quick squirt, followed by a wipe-down with a damp cloth. Miraculously, it worked a treat, only leaving a faint trace of ink. I suppose I should add a disclaimer here – what works for me may not work for others – but that can of hairspray is now kept permanently in my utility room, to deal with future Sharpie marks. I'm quite proud of my little household hack; maybe I should share it on Instagram . . .

* * *

I have an 'all hands on deck' policy in my household. As soon as my children are able to walk, they're encouraged to do various jobs around the home, whether that's polishing their shoes, emptying their bins or tidying their toys. My domestic workload is huge nowadays – only to be expected with a family of eight – but, if the kids pull their weight, that daily grind becomes slightly more manageable. Every little helps.

I'm not the only beneficiary of this muck-in attitude, of course. I'm very keen for my sons and daughters to learn practical skills at an early age, as this encourages independence in later life. As grown adults, they need to have the ability to stand on their own two feet and, by asking them to help around the house, I'm preparing them for the road ahead. It's something I feel really passionately about. I hear far too many stories about young people unprepared for life outside their family unit and lacking basic skills – some are barely able to boil an egg or iron a shirt. I know for sure that, when the time comes for them to fly the nest, my kids will be savvy and self-reliant.

All my children are given their own tasks to fulfil, indoors and outdoors. Because she spends a good deal of time at home, Venezuela has the biggest to-do list. As well as sharing the morning chores with me, she'll often take care of her baby sister Athena, as well as minding the other younger siblings if need be. My eldest daughter is very mature for her age, with lots of common sense, so is more than capable of making the other kids' lunch or keeping them occupied in the garden. Helping out like this might benefit her own future, too. One day Venezuela might want children of her own, and all this practice will give her a decent bank of knowledge and experience. She should be very well-equipped to cope with sulks, strops and tantrums.

As he nears his teens, Prince does his fair share of jobs, too. It's his responsibility to keep my and Tyson's cars clean, inside and out, so at weekends he's often found on the driveway, armed with his bucket and sponge. Since he's a well-built lad, he's also on hand to help carry any heavy or bulky items around the house; he will help me haul big bags of toys or laundry up and down the stairs, or assist with our weighty suitcases if I need to load them into the van. Other than little Athena (who's still a bit too young to join our mini-workforce) the rest of the children also do their bit. Little Tyson will help me set the table, Valencia will help me tidy the play area and Adonis will help me pair the socks. They might take twenty minutes to finish a job I'd usually whizz through in ten, but that's neither here nor there. For me, it's the principle of the matter. It's about lending a hand and learning new skills.

Sometimes, we all pitch in together to get a job done. Clearing up after teatime is a prime example. When we've finished eating our meal, I'll say, 'Venezuela, collect

161

the plates . . . Valencia, grab the cutlery . . . Prince, load the dishwasher . . .' Meanwhile, I'll wipe down the table and surfaces, while Little Tyson puts the sauce bottles back into the cupboard and Adonis stacks the placemats nice and neatly. This family effort ensures the job gets done quickly and efficiently. It's like one big assembly line.

If Big Tyson is at home, usually between fights, he'll happily tackle a chore or two. I'll often ask him to take out the bins, vacuum the carpets or jet-wash the driveway. Whenever Tyson's around, you can virtually guarantee the house being super-tidy. Having OCD, he hates any clutter and disorder – it totally stresses him out – and he'll leap out of his chair to sweep up any dropped food or to tidy up the kids' toys.

Some people might assume that everyday domestic duties are a comedown for a champion boxer, but that's certainly not the case with Tyson. He enjoys leading a normal life, out of the public eye and away from the media spotlight. To us, our home is our special little sanctuary, a 'happy place' where we can be ourselves, recharge our batteries and relax with our loved ones. Will we stay in Morecambe forever? It's a question we often ask ourselves. I don't think Gypsies ever feel truly settled in one place – there's always an urge to travel, in my case – so there could well be more house moves in the future.

We might even choose to live abroad for a while, who knows – but as things stand, we're happy to stay put. To be honest, as long as my beloved family are beside me, I really don't care where I live. Home is where the heart is, as they say. It isn't my house that brings me joy and happiness, it's the people within.

CHAPTER SEVEN

HAVE KIDS ... WILL TRAVEL

I LOVE A holiday in the sun – who doesn't? – although getting the super-sized Fury family from A to B can be pretty challenging, whether it's cramming everything we need into three or four suitcases or keeping the children entertained during flights. But, with years of practice and experience behind me, I think I've nearly cracked it. For starters, I don't let the prospect of travelling en masse hold me back, whether we're travelling short-haul or long-haul (having holidayed in Europe and the USA, we've done both). And I've also realised that being super-organised is crucial if things are to run as smoothly as possible. These days, I'm able to pack all our bags with my eyes closed (well, almost) and I have a few canny tricks up my sleeve that work like a dream in airports and on aeroplanes. Who knows – some of them might work for you and your family.

I reckon all hard-working mams and dads need a break

from the normal routine of chores and childcare. For me, the thought of a *whole week* without cooking, cleaning or doing the school run almost makes me want to jump for joy. Having a change of scenery now and then is always a good idea in my book, even if it's just a trip to the beach or a walk in the woods. I know I function much better as a parent when I've had some time away from the same-old, same-old. Going on holiday enables me to unwind (well, as much as I can with small kids in tow) and, in an ideal world, allows me to return home feeling nicely relaxed and refreshed.

I'm a big fan of travelling and sightseeing. I love visiting new places and sampling other cultures, and count myself lucky that Tyson's career has taken me all over the world, from Dubai to Miami, and from the Swiss Alps to the French Riviera. I was born with itchy feet and a restless nature, just like my own mother who, as a youngster, travelled all over the United States with her parents. In fact, I take a lot of inspiration from Mam's get-up-and-go mindset. When we were kids she always encouraged us to broaden our horizons through travel and exploration, and took us on plenty of fun-filled trips, both home and abroad. 'A going foot always gets something, even if it's only a blister,' she used to say, echoing the words of my Granny Mary.

Our family holidays often come shortly after one of

Tyson's title fights. By then, he's desperate for some downtime – the whole process is physically and emotionally draining – and jetting off to the sun becomes his top priority. Me and the kids are equally keen to get away from it all. The children miss their dad terribly while he's at training camp, and can't wait to have him all to themselves again. And, having spent the run-up to the fight plagued with stress and worry, I'm more than happy to escape the world of boxing for a while.

* * *

As a rule, the job of booking our getaways is delegated to Tyson, which I'm quite glad about because I'm completely useless with computers. He has a tendency, however, to suddenly spring things on me, giving me days (or some-times hours) to get everything packed and ready. I think the most notice he's given me is a fortnight. Not long ago he finished booking a holiday online at 11 p.m., and by 2 p.m. the following day we were all sat on a plane, flying out to Tenerife. Tyson's spur-of-the-moment attitude means I'm in a constant state of alert, poised for the moment he receives a confirmation email and says, 'Go get the suitcases, Paris, we're off . . .'

I can understand why these last-minute-Charlie antics

might drive other women crazy, but I've become used to it. It's all part and parcel of being married to Tyson Fury. He doesn't live a normal nine-to-five life – he never has – and, unless there's a big fight on the horizon, he rarely plans ahead. Everything's done on the hoof. But I've learned to just go with the flow. With Tyson, I've come to expect the unexpected.

As soon as our holiday is confirmed I'll set to my task, like I'm on autopilot. I'll grab one suitcase for the girls, one suitcase for the boys, and another one for me and Tyson to share. For each child, I'll pack eight pairs of pants, socks and vests, plus three sets of pyjamas. I'll take enough items for them to have ten changes of clothing during the holiday, so plenty of mix-and-match T-shirts, shorts and skirts, and perhaps a couple of nice outfits for evenings out. And, finally, I'll throw in the all-important swimwear and sunhats.

More often than not, I'll do a laundry wash at the halfway point of the holiday so there's no risk of running out of clean and fresh clothes. I try to give myself a break from household chores (especially if we have a cleaner) but this is one of the few exceptions. I couldn't bear my kids running around the complex in grubby clothes.

I try to limit the number of children's shoes – they take up too much suitcase space – so that usually means a pair of comfy trainers to walk around in, and a pair of Crocs or flip-flops for the pool. Being a fashion-conscious teenager, however, Venezuela wants to take dozens of shoes and dressy outfits. For this reason, I let her pack her own small suitcase, although I always give it a final once-over to check she's not gone totally OTT for a week-long holiday.

'I was a teenager once, you know,' I'll laugh, holding up a glittery minidress. 'I totally get that you want to look nice – just don't overdo it.'

My and Tyson's suitcase is the easiest to pack, since most of our holiday attire will already be hanging up in wardrobes, having been washed and ironed straight after our previous break. My husband doesn't mind me packing his holiday gear and is quite happy when I take over. After fourteen years of marriage I know exactly what he'll want to put in his suitcase. As well as his usual daywear, I'll pack some smart outfits for the evening, which usually includes a couple of his favourite Versace shirts (he's amassed a great collection over the years).

As for me, in addition to the usual shorts, sarongs and swimwear I might take two or three summery dresses, ideal for when we eat out at local restaurants. There's a good chance they'll have been bought from high street stores.

Wherever possible I prefer to stick to cotton-rich clothing – it's such a light material to pack – and, to save more suitcase space, I'll encourage the family to travel in bulky items like hoodies, sweatshirts and joggers (which also act as useful extra layers if it gets chilly or breezy at night). I know some people swear by tightly rolling their clothes into long sausage shapes, so they can squash everything in and reduce creases. I prefer not to do this, though. I like to fold my items as flat as I can, in the conventional way, with only one crease line. So I'm more Team Folder than Team Roller, but each to their own. Like most things, do whatever works for you!

On the actual day of departure, once all the suitcases are packed and secured it's time to ensure all our holiday admin is ready. I'm usually pretty organised in this respect; with so many of us, I simply can't be slapdash. So I guard the all-important passports with my life – they're stored safely in the backpack I use for hand luggage – and Tyson looks after the tickets, passes and insurance documents, which, as is usually the case these days, are stored on his phone. I'd much rather deal with paper tickets rather than e-tickets, but I have to accept that time and technology have moved on. When we're good to go, we'll drive our minibus to the airport – either Manchester or Liverpool – and leave it in one of the secure car parks. Then, once we arrive at the terminal, the most challenging stage of our travels will begin.

I don't think we're the only parents who dread the whole palaver of going through security and passport control. All those necessary checks and procedures can be incredibly stressful, especially when you have lots of children to supervise, and even more so when your husband is a world-famous boxer. The Fury family always attracts lots of attention from airport staff and fellow passengers – sometimes you feel people are watching your every move – but Tyson and I have learned to blank it out and just focus on the children.

Tyson used to find the whole airport procedure unbearable – the plastic trays, the conveyor belts, the security scanners – largely because it triggered his OCD. He craves order and discipline in his life, and being shunted through security amid swarms of tourists, all stressing out and jostling for space, became totally overwhelming for him. As we attempted to herd the kids through the system, trying to keep tabs on them all, I'd notice his anxiety levels rising, and his breathing getting heavier. On one occasion I had to have a quiet word, in an attempt to calm him down.

'Listen, I know this is stressful for you, Tyson, but you've just got to try and get through the next half-hour,'

I whispered. 'Then we can relax in the departure lounge with a nice cup of coffee.'

Tyson copes much better nowadays, thankfully. He has learned to focus on the lovely holiday ahead rather than the hassle beforehand.

When we eventually get through security, I'll head over to Boots to buy a family pack of sun cream. This contains a variety of SPFs to cater for all of us, ranging from factor 15 for me and Tyson to total sunblock for the babies and toddlers. In fact, I hardly pack any toiletries in our hold luggage – they add far too much weight – and I only purchase basics like soap, shampoo or shower gel when I arrive at the resort (and they're often cheaper when bought locally, in any case). I keep any vital medicines in a miniature first aid box that I'll pop into my backpack. This includes antihistamine tablets for Prince's food allergies, and liquid paracetamol should the kids suffer with mid-flight earache.

Controlling a handful of excitable and energetic kids at an airport isn't easy, especially if the flight has been delayed. But I have a couple of little tricks that work a treat. Firstly, on the day of departure I only let the kids snack on crisps or fruit, and keep them away from any sweets or fizzy drinks. So no Haribos or Coca-Cola at all. If I let them overdose on sugar they'll only get hyperactive, and are much more likely to create havoc in the airport and annoy fellow passengers.

Secondly, I'll try to find a quiet corner of the airport where the children can play safely. If I have a wander, I'll almost always find a deserted departure gate that we can use for that purpose. I often pop a sponge ball into my backpack so they can have a game of catch (not football, though – that would be asking for trouble). Not only does this keep them entertained, it also tires them out, so they're more likely to drop off during the flight. I'm quite proud of these top tips, if I say so myself. Feel free to steal them . . .!

* * *

Flying with small children in tow can be incredibly hit and miss, in my experience. The outward journey might work like a dream, with every one of them behaving impeccably, yet the return journey might be an absolute nightmare, with moans, groans and meltdowns wherever I turn. Kids are unpredictable by nature and, while you're cooped up in an aeroplane, especially if we're flying long-haul, it's often a case of crossing your fingers, saying a quick prayer and hoping for the best. But I do think it's important to manage your expectations and take pressure off yourself. Despite all your efforts, you may not be able to control how your children are going to behave during the flight, especially if they're at the baby or toddler stage.

If any of my little ones kick up a fuss on the plane, I do my utmost to soothe and settle them, which might mean handing them their dummy or reading them a story. And I try my best to ignore any disapproving looks. There's almost always one passenger who'll loudly tut or raise their eyebrows, the implication being you're a hopeless mother who can't control your child. But I do find that most fellow parents – especially those with young kids – are very understanding in these situations, because they've been through similar themselves. The cabin crew are usually very helpful and sympathetic, too. I'd never dream of making another mam or dad feel uncomfortable if they were struggling on a flight. Coping with an agitated child is bad enough as it is, without being judged by others. In those instances, I always try to put myself in someone else's shoes and imagine how they must be feeling.

Keeping kids amused and entertained on a flight can be hard – especially if you've got two rows to look after – but an element of forward planning can be a good idea. My hand luggage (and Tyson's) is always packed full of things to occupy their minds. We always ensure the younger ones have plenty of pens, pencils and colouring books as well as a couple of comfort toys to cuddle, like their favourite dolls or teddies. We never forget to pack the iPads and Nintendo devices for the older kids, who'll kill time by playing video games or watching movies and cartoons. But they have to wear their headsets or keep the volume to a minimum. Years ago, a woman sitting in front of us complained about the bleeps and pings coming from the kids' gadgets. You could barely hear them, but she clearly had a big problem with it.

'Do you mind, I'm trying to do some work,' she said, which was like showing a red rag to a bull.

'I think you'll find it's an aeroplane, not an office,' I replied.

I was being a bit cheeky, I admit, but I thought she was making a mountain out of a mole hill, because the kids were actually being as good as gold; maybe *she* should have worn the headphones if she had important work to do.

We've occasionally flown first class as a family, too, usually when we're travelling over to America. Tyson's six-foot-nine frame needs plenty of legroom when we're up in the air for that length of time. But, if I'm honest, when we're flying with kids I'm much happier in economy class. The 'posh' seats are lovely, don't get me wrong – in fact, they're more like beds than seats – but they're spaced so far apart I can hardly reach the children.

Whenever we travel economy, there's a specific family seating plan. If we've got a baby in tow, like Athena, they'll usually sit on Tyson's knee. I'll have the little ones either side of me, Valencia and Adonis, so I can easily keep them entertained with their toys and books. Tyson and I will often swap places, though, especially when the baby needs feeding or changing. Sitting across the aisle will be the older kids, Venezuela, Prince and Little Tyson; this way, they can swap and share their iPads and devices.

But in first class, it's much harder to tap the children on the shoulder if they're being naughty or to hold their hands if they need reassurance, hence me preferring economy. I doubt my kids agree with me – they love being treated like rock stars – but I'd prefer not to get into the habit of luxury travel. For me, it's a matter of principle. I don't want to end up with a bunch of entitled sons and daughters who automatically turn left whenever they board a plane. That's just not real life. Not only that, the passengers in those de luxe seats spend serious money for the privilege and might not appreciate sharing their space with a load of youngsters. My kids are well behaved on the whole but, like most curious and mischievous children, they can't help flicking the light switches and pressing the recliner buttons. It's the least relaxing experience for me – I'm forever on edge – so give me economy class any day of the week . . .

Flying with tiny babies requires a lot of preparation. I should know; I've done it plenty of times, most notably with Little Tyson, Valencia and Adonis, when all three were less than a few months old. I've never let their tender age hold me back. 'Have kids . . . will travel,' is my motto. In fact, some might argue it's more straightforward to fly with newborns because they're easier to pacify when they're snuggled in your arms. But even if you're blessed with a very well-behaved baby, there are certain things you can do to make everything run as smoothly as possible. Making up the baby's bottles beforehand goes without saying, of course, but I always take along a couple of extra cartons of ready-to-use milk in case it's needed.

The special baby backpack (which Venezuela is often tasked with carrying, because Tyson and I have our hands full) also contains a change of clothing – a pair of basic babygrows, maybe – in the event of any sick or poo splurges. Other essentials include bibs, nappies and muslin squares, as well as a fluffy blanket to use if the cabin temperature dips. And if I think my baby is struggling with the air pressure during landing or take-off – the clue is in the crying – I'll give them their bottle or their dummy to suck, which helps to ease earache, I'm told.

I've travelled alone with babies before now, and coped pretty well single-handedly, but I much prefer Tyson to be around. This way, we can share the load, passing children to and fro to give each other a break. We might take it in turns to walk our baby up and down the aisle, rocking them in our arms, the hope being that the motion will eventually soothe them (although it's important to get the timing right, as getting trapped behind the drinks trolley is never a good move). But however we choose to manage things, Tyson and I try to stay cool, calm and collected. A crying baby is a perfectly normal part of life – it's what they do! – and sometimes we just have to ride the storm and count down the minutes until landing.

I've also flown a few times while pregnant. This included a flight to Amsterdam while carrying Little Tyson in 2016 (Big Tyson was training in Holland at the time) and a flight to Las Vegas, while expecting Adonis, to watch the second Fury versus Wilder showdown in 2018. I take medical advice from health professionals before I travel, without exception, and make sure I get all the appropriate checks and certificates. If a doctor ever advised me not to fly, for the sake of my own health or the baby's, I'd definitely take heed and stay put. But so far I've been given the all-clear on every occasion, on the proviso that I take all the necessary precautions.

So looking after myself during the flight is paramount when I'm expecting. First and foremost, I'll drink plenty of water to stay hydrated and to prevent any nausea.

Food-wise, I try not to put too much strain on my stomach, so will just nibble some snacks or eat a very light meal. I'll also practise some circulation-boosting exercises, as recommended by my midwife, which generally involve leg stretches while I sit, as well as regular walkabouts up and down the aisle to keep my blood pumping.

Dressing comfortably is important, too – you don't want to feel too restricted – so I'll normally wear a stretchy tracksuit and some cushioned trainers. The sort of outfit I usually do my housework in, so casual but smart. I might also put on a pair of compression flight socks; not the most attractive items of clothing, granted, but they apparently reduce the likelihood of deep vein thrombosis (DVT) and other circulation issues. It's always something to be mindful of; better safe than sorry.

*   *   *

To keep everybody happy, our ideal family summer holiday needs to meet certain criteria. Since there's so many of us, this is easier said than done. The destination itself is very important, of course, and we usually plump for somewhere hot, but not *too* hot. Being a big sun worshipper, I'd bake in forty-plus degrees if I could – I love blisteringly hot weather – but Tyson begs to differ.

He prefers the temperature to be warm rather than blazing, so hot enough to go in the pool, but not too hot to walk around without dripping in sweat. As a compromise, we'll often opt for the Canary Islands or the Costa del Sol, which both have fairly short flight times and tend not to be as stifling as places like Turkey or Cyprus (although that's not always the case – we've had a few Spanish sizzlers in the past!).

One resort that ticks all our boxes is Cannes, the beautiful city in the South of France. Tyson and I have been visiting for years, ever since he attended a nearby training camp, and it's become one of our favourite places in Europe (and the children now love it, too). I'm drawn to its coastline and climate – springtime is particularly gorgeous in Cannes – as well as the amazing shops and restaurants. The chilled-out way of life on the French Riviera really appeals to me, too – *la belle vie*, as they say in French – and I like the fact it's not jam-packed with holidaymakers. There's such a lovely, relaxed vibe over there. The minute I set foot in this happy place, any stress just flows away. I like to visit every year if I can.

Last summer, Tyson and I hired out a family-sized yacht in Nice for a few days. The children thought it was fabulous, and loved sailing out to sea and taking part in water sports. Everything's really safe – life-vests have to be worn at all times – but I still keep an extra-close eye on all their activities. So while it may not be a totally relaxing time for me during the day, I'll make up for it in the evening when the kids are tucked up in bed. Then, Tyson and I can chill out on the deck together, enjoying the views of Nice by night.

So as far as we're concerned, the perfect holiday is a good combination of sunbathing and sightseeing. We like to discover the local area, not just stay inside the tourist bubble, so much prefer to choose resorts that have some history attached to them; maybe a place where we can tour ancient castles and cathedrals, visit museums and explore quaint old towns and villages. The younger children have a short attention span, though – they get easily bored – but that doesn't stop our family having the odd day trip, as a change from the pool and the beach. I think it's good for the kids to do some sight-seeing, but no doubt they'll appreciate it more when they're older. To be fair, I don't remember being a massive fan of castles and cathedrals when I was a teenager . . .

Occasionally, Tyson and I will ask my mam and dad to join us on holiday, which is a lovely experience for us all. Not only do we really enjoy their company – they're both very laid-back and easy-going – we also massively appreciate their kind offers to babysit. My parents adore their grandchildren (and vice versa) and are more than happy to hold the fort so my husband and I can go out for the evening. The perfect win-win situation. It's great to spend some time on our own; there's nothing more romantic than sitting with your soulmate in a beachside bistro, with a glass of something nice, and watching the sun go down. My idea of heaven.

*   *   *

The type of accommodation is another important consideration when we book a getaway. In the past, Tyson has usually opted for a large villa with a pool and sun terrace. It's an ideal choice for the family because it's spacious enough to cater for the whole clan (including Mam and Dad, if they're with us) and also allows us plenty of privacy and security, away from crowds and tourists. This option also means that other families are able to join us. Before now, close friends of ours have booked a neighbouring villa, which means the kids can all play together and, once they're tucked up in bed, us adults can relax with a few drinks on the terrace.

A couple of years ago we rented a fabulous mansion in Florida, complete with a cinema room, a bowling alley and a play area, which I thought would tick everybody's boxes. It turned out I was wrong.

'Did you like the villa, then?' I said to my eldest son Prince, as our week in the sun came to a close.

'It was really nice, Mam,' he said, 'but it got a little bit boring after a while. There was no one for me to hang out with.'

He had a point. Being the eldest boy, he'd often had to visit the bowling alley alone because it wasn't Venezuela's 'thing', the other kids were too young, and Tyson often had his hands full, running around after the toddlers. And the villa was a little off the beaten track, so Prince had felt a little isolated.

But our son's honest words gave me and Tyson food for thought, and when the time came to book our next family holiday we decided to change tack. Instead of a villa we opted for a big hotel complex in the Canary Islands, which boasted an array of lively amenities for Prince and Venezuela but also had plenty of activities for the little ones. And guess what – the children had a blast. They made friends with loads of kids on the complex – the young Furys are a sociable and approachable lot – and they said the on-site fun and games were 'awesome'. Prince took part in the football camps during the day – he's sports mad – and both he and Venezuela loved going to the hotel discos at night. The middle children – Valencia, Little Tyson and Adonis – popped in and out of the holiday clubs, too, which allowed me to spend some extra time with Tyson and baby Athena.

I'll be honest, it wasn't the ideal holiday for us parents, but on this occasion we were willing to put the kids' needs before ours; we certainly didn't want them to miss out on having great experiences with other similarly aged children. Staying in a busy hotel complex means that Tyson and I will inevitably sacrifice some privacy, but this is a price worth paying if it keeps the children happy. Our fellow holidaymakers are pretty respectful, on the whole. They understand Tyson is off duty, as such – like most dads, he craves quality time with his family – and they'll only ask him for a selfie when he's not with me and the children, perhaps when he's walking to the shop or sitting with a friend in the bar. And, once his fans have got the picture they want, they'll leave him alone for the rest of the holiday.

Not everyone is quite so considerate, though. Some people won't think twice about bothering him while he's by the pool with the kids and, once one person does that, others will cotton on and a queue will suddenly form. Then Tyson will have to gently explain that this is neither the time nor the place, but that he'll gladly oblige in the bar later. He always approaches these situations in a firm but fair manner, without causing any fuss. It's the best way to be.

Other times, sadly, people have sneakily filmed us on their phones as we're swimming or sunbathing. I don't think any woman would like her bikini body being uploaded to social media, or published by a newspaper (which has happened to me in the past), and I'm no exception. I'd much rather people kept their mobiles in their beach bags than train them on me. I'm no super-model striking a pose by the pool, drawing attention to myself; I'm just trying to enjoy some normal time in the sun with my family. I do find it quite intrusive and disrespectful.

So whether we choose to holiday with the family in a villa or a hotel, I can't say it's ever a *totally* relaxing experience for me. Not that I'd ever expect it to be the case anyway, with all the kids to look after – but then again I knew what I signed up for when I decided to have so many! So any idea I may have of lazing around the pool all day, sipping cocktails and reading *Vogue*, goes straight out of the window. It's just not my real-ity. Whenever we're on holiday I've always got one eye on the swimming pool or the sun terrace, either check-ing that the kids are wearing their water wings or worrying that they're wearing enough sun protection. Luckily Prince and Venezuela are old enough to not require constant monitoring, but they have different demands.

'Mam, can we have five euros for an ice cream?' they'll ask.

'Here's ten,' I'll reply, handing them a note. 'Get me and your dad one, too.'

I do get some respite, though. Just like at home, Tyson and I will split the childcare – he might keep a couple of the young ones occupied, while I look after the others – but we also try to allow ourselves a little bit of 'me-time'. Each morning, Tyson will head off for a run or a workout (a decent gym is another holiday must-have) but when he returns, he'll give me a breather for an hour or so. I might go for a swim, grab myself a coffee, or lie on my sunlounger. Whatever I do, I'll relish every single moment of that peace and tranquillity. It's a rarity for me these days.

*   *   *

Most of our summer holidays take place abroad rather than at home. This is down to the weather more than anything else. I love basking in the sun when I go away – it gives me a tan and lifts my spirits – and that just can't be guaranteed in the UK. We've discovered this to our cost. We once booked a summer holiday at a popular park resort in England that turned into a total disaster. It bucketed with rain the whole time, which in turn restricted many of the outdoor activities and put more onus on us to entertain a handful of kids, all of whom wanted to do different things. Tyson and I were at our wits' end by the end of the week – we were emotionally and physically shattered – and we couldn't wait to pack our bags and go home. Not only that, the holiday cost us a fortune (twice as much as we'd pay for a foreign trip) because we didn't realise that lots of activities were charged as extras. We may be comfortably off, but we've both been brought up to expect decent value for money, whether it's a product, a service or an experience. And this certainly wasn't it.

'That's the first and last time we do that,' said Tyson as we drove home to Morecambe, feeling damp and downbeat.

'Agreed,' I replied. 'I think I need another holiday to recover . . .'

Far cheaper (and more enjoyable, if I'm honest) were the motorhome holidays we took a few years ago, when we only had three or four children in tow. Tyson and I hired a big six-berth campervan and drove down to Devon and Cornwall – a truly lovely part of the world – but our five-day tour of Scotland was my favourite road trip by far. We visited the stunning area of Loch Ness, in the Scottish Highlands, accompanied by my father-in-law. It was great to spend some time with Big John – he's brilliant company, and is a lovely grandad to the kids – and the scenery we passed through was utterly breathtaking. This mini-break also brought back some happy memories of my own childhood. When I was a girl, we crossed the border on many occasions to visit family – I come from a long line of Scots – and, ever since then, I've felt a real connection with the country.

I'd love to spend more time in Scotland, although I'm not sure another motorhome holiday would suit me at the moment. We'd need a jumbo Winnebago to cater for our growing family and, with so many of us vying for space, I imagine it being complete chaos. Having said that, I can imagine Tyson and me doing another campervan road trip someday, but certainly not while we have so many kids to look after. We really fancy touring Italy together – it seems such a beautiful country – and would particularly love to explore Rome, Florence and Pompeii.

I'm a big fan of a Great British day out, too. Mam used to arrange some lovely little jaunts for me and my siblings, and I'm carrying on that tradition with my own kids (and Tyson, if he's around). Like my mother, though, I rarely organise these trips in advance. Our family isn't really into forward planning. Ninety per cent of the time, we Furys don't know what we're doing from one weekend to the next – everything's on the hoof – and on a Saturday or Sunday morning we'll just decide there and then what's on the agenda, depending on how we feel or how the weather's looking. But we'll invariably do some sort of activity or other, whether it's going for a hike or a cycle. We're not the sort of family that lazes around the house all weekend. We like to get up and go.

The children like Blackpool most of all. We live quite nearby – it's a forty-minute drive away – and we probably take a trip every couple of months, often with cousins or friends of the family. Tyson usually decides to stay at home, though; when we've visited previously he's been mobbed by fans, which isn't always ideal for the kids.

'Aw, Dad's not coming to Blackpool, is he?' Prince once said, when we were planning a birthday party for him in the resort. It's nothing against Tyson – the kids love spending time with their dad – but, whenever he's with us, it puts a whole different complexion on the outing. Now and again I'll attract a few points and stares ('Ooh, isn't that Paris Fury?') but it's nothing like the attention Tyson receives.

Blackpool is a children's paradise. There's so much to do. We usually make a beeline for the Pleasure Beach, where the older kids can scare themselves silly on the ghost train or the Big Dipper, and the younger ones can opt for the calmer rides in Nickelodeon Land. All the children love Coral Island, a huge amusements complex where they can spend their pocket money on arcade games and fruit machines. Then there's the waxworks in Madame Tussauds, the Blackpool Tower Dungeon, and – when it's time for refreshments – a great, child-friendly beachside restaurant. The weather can be hit and miss (we're talking the north-west of England here!) but in summer I always load buckets and spades into the boot, just in case we're blessed with a sunny afternoon. There's nothing like a good old-fashioned day at the seaside when the sun has got its hat on.

We have lots of family trips to the countryside, too. We're not far from some lovely beauty spots – the Lake District and the Forest of Bowland are only half an hour's drive away – so you can easily find yourself in the middle of nowhere, with no other soul in sight. The open space and the lack of crowds is ideal for Tyson, of course, as he can totally relax and be a normal dad. He's never happier than when he's walking along a river or exploring a forest, sometimes with a baby strapped to his back or with a toddler in a buggy. Like me, he's a big nature lover and will stop along the way to point out a landmark or some wildlife that might interest the children; an old ruin, perhaps, or a bird of prey.

We'll sometimes take picnics with us, especially in the summer. I'll either knock up a stack of roast chicken sandwiches at home beforehand or, if I'm pressed for time, stop off at the supermarket to grab a selection of food and drink. We'll occasionally meet up with Tyson's brother Shane and his wife Helen, and will locate a scenic spot where the children can all play safely. We never picnic at the seaside – sand, food and kids don't mix, in my experience – so we usually head up to a place like Windermere, in the South Lakes, which is blessed with some of the most beautiful views in the area. The younger cousins always have a whale of a time in the fresh air, running around and playing hide-and-seek, while the older ones often prefer to chill out in the picnic chairs, chatting away with the grown-ups. I cherish this quality time. It's all about making memories. Each outing or holiday is like a little story that I can keep forever.

So, while travelling with a clutch of young children has its challenges, I think all the effort and upheaval is well worth it. Having a change of scenery and a break from everyday life – even for a week – makes a huge difference to our family's well-being. In fact, Tyson is probably booking our next sunshine trip right now. I'd better get those suitcases ready . . .

Chapter Eight

BEING KIND TO MYSELF

In order to function properly, I think it's vital that we busy mams look after our mental and physical well-being. Now and then we all need a break from the hustle and bustle of family life, no matter how old our children are, and grabbing some me-time – even just a pit stop for coffee – can feel like a breath of fresh air. And we certainly shouldn't feel guilty for taking time out to relax, unwind and focus on ourselves. From my experience, the more balance I have in my life the better mother I am. If I'm caring for myself properly, and feeling refreshed and energised, I find I'm much more patient and productive. On the other hand, if I'm feeling frazzled and run-down, it can be much harder to get through the day.

Being a mam can feel like the hardest job in the world – you wear so many hats and spin so many plates – and it's easy to feel weary and overwhelmed. In my crazy life, there never seem to be enough hours in the day (and the weeks just seem to fly by), which means that prioritising any time for myself can be difficult. Like most dutiful parents, I sacrifice a lot for my kids, and their needs always come before mine. That's part and parcel of motherhood. But as much as I love my children, it's really important I take care of myself, too.

Finding that extra time is tricky, however. Sometimes your own needs are shunted down the list of priorities, especially when you're facing challenges in your family life. Tyson's two-year battle with mental illness and alcohol addiction, not long after his 2015 victory over Wladimir Klitschko, was a case in point. It was an incredibly testing time for me. The anxiety and worry was never-ending. Tyson's depression badly affected his mood and behaviour – he didn't even seem to care that I was pregnant with our fourth child – and our relationship suffered terribly as a result. I became so preoccupied with supporting Tyson in his hour of need, shielding three young children from all the trauma, that I completely lost sight of my own well-being. A lack of me-time was the least of my worries when I had a husband who was experiencing depression, paranoia and suicidal thoughts.

But I look back now and realise that, even under all that strain, I somehow managed to cope. I kept the household going, gave birth to my beautiful daughter Valencia and helped Tyson get himself back on track. I do wonder, though, how on earth I got through this miserable time with barely any respite. Back then, I rejected offers of help from family and friends (wrongly, in hindsight) because I felt I could plough on alone. I thought I'd be a burden on my loved ones. But all this turmoil and upheaval weighed heavily on me, and it took a long time for me to get back to my old self, and for our family life to feel 'normal' again.

Tyson is in a much better place these days, touch wood – and our marriage was strong enough to survive – but this unhappy episode taught me a life lesson. When your world seems to be falling apart, you need to be as kind to yourself as you are to others. In troubled times, you should talk to your nearest and dearest – a problem shared is always a problem halved – and accept any emotional or practical help when it's offered. Never again will I struggle alone. The responses to my first book, *Love & Fury*, made me realise that I wasn't the only person to suffer in this way. Other wives and husbands got in touch, telling me that they'd gone through similar crises and hadn't known where to turn while their partners suffered emotional breakdowns. By opening up about my own experiences, I'd given them the strength to seek help. This was so comforting to hear.

Indulging in some me-time is also easier said than done when you have young children to care for. In fact, it's pretty much impossible when you have a newborn attached to you like a limpet, plus two demanding toddlers, as I did a few years ago when I had Adonis as well as Valencia (who was only two) and Little Tyson (who was three). That was also at a time when Tyson was often training abroad for weeks on end, leaving me to hold the fort alone. To keep myself going, I grabbed any spare moments I could. In the afternoon, when the little ones were asleep, I'd try to snatch a twenty-minute nap. In the evening, when the kids were tucked up in bed, I'd run myself a nice, hot bath. I'd pour in my favourite bubbles, turn the lights down low and have a long soak, enjoying the peace, quiet and relaxation. I always felt so much better afterwards. Luxuriating in the bath remains one of my favourite treats. Those simple little things can make all the difference.

Practising good self-care also means taking the pressure off yourself. Occasionally I'll have one of those crazy, chaotic days at home when the kids are being super-demanding and I can't find the time to complete my list of household chores. But when I feel my stress levels rising I'll have a quiet word with myself.

Surely cleaning the windows can wait 'til tomorrow, Paris? a little voice in my head will say. *You've been running around after the kids since breakfast. You've done your bit. Have a coffee and a Hobnob. And don't you dare feel guilty about it . . .*

So I'll sit down for ten minutes and enjoy my drink and biscuit. And the following day, I'll clean those windows until they sparkle.

* * *

With such a busy lifestyle, it's really important I keep myself in good physical shape. With so many kids to look after, especially my lively little preschoolers, I need plenty of energy and stamina to get me through the day. Since becoming a wife and mam I've hardly stopped, whether it's pushing babies around parks, rushing up and down supermarket aisles or whizzing around the house with a vacuum cleaner. This constant to-ing and fro-ing must have burned plenty of calories over the years. I don't hang about. In fact, I once tried out an exercise tracker watch for a few weeks and discovered I was regularly clocking up more than ten miles per day just going about my usual business.

And, while I'm naturally fit and active, I wouldn't say I'm a particularly sporty person. I never have been. When I was growing up on Tilts Farm, my little sister Montana was forever running, cycling or playing football but, other than a few trips to the swimming pool, I wasn't very interested. I was by no means lazy, of course, and kept busy in other ways, from playing in the nearby woods to assisting Mam with the household chores. Being busy was my only real exercise and I didn't set foot in a gym until my mid-twenties; I just didn't see the appeal of working out.

I'm not a big spectator of sport, either, and don't follow anything on TV, like rugby or football. The only boxing fights I watch in person are those that feature Tyson, and even then it's more out of duty than enjoyment. Believe me, I don't relish seeing my husband getting punched in the face for a living but, as his wife, I don't think twice about supporting him from my ringside seat. My prime concern is his health and safety – it's such a risky and dangerous sport – and it goes without saying that I'm the most relieved person in the stadium when Tyson emerges from the bout unscathed. For me, any victory is an added bonus.

As an elite athlete, Tyson spends hours training in the gym, or his 'second home' as I like to call it. This strict regime helps keep him physically and mentally conditioned, giving him the routine and discipline he needs in life. I witnessed his commitment to the cause for myself during the coronavirus lockdown, when our front room became Tyson's makeshift gym. He roped me into taking part in his morning cardiovascular workouts, which he broadcast over Instagram to thousands of people around the world. It was his unique way of keeping everyone's spirits up, as well as his own. At first I didn't take his punishing fitness routine too seriously – it was just something to relieve the boredom – but, as the weeks went by, I began to really enjoy it. And, much to my surprise, the results were amazing. I don't think my body had ever been so trim and toned. I felt brilliant.

There were lots of laughs to be had on camera, but there were plenty of sulks and strops, too. I have a feeling that's why so many people tuned in, to see us bickering and back-biting like any other married couple. It was Tyson's tough taskmaster attitude that caused the most friction, though. He expected me, a stay-at-home mam, to keep pace with him, a world-class sportsman. I dug as deep as I could – *you're not going to break me, Tyson Fury*, I'd say to myself – but whenever I started to flag, he'd get impatient and irritable.

'C'mon, Paris, keep up, you're letting the side down . . .' he'd moan, while performing his fiftieth sit-up.

'You do realise I'm not an Olympic athlete, Tyson?' I'd say, as I took a well-earned breather. 'Give me a break, will you?'

Our social media sessions came to a natural end after lockdown. Tyson resumed training at his Morecambe gym and I returned to my usual morning routine, namely getting the kids fed, dressed and ready for school. In many ways I missed our daily workouts. They'd made me feel better, inside and out, and I'd become quite proud of my streamlined physique.

It wasn't until the following year, a few months after Athena was born, that I decided to start exercising again. As I hit my thirties, I couldn't help but notice that I was carrying a bit more weight than usual and was finding it harder to shift those extra post-pregnancy pounds. I felt my energy levels were dipping, too. So I enrolled at the local gym, along with my good friend Marylouise who was in a similar boat to me. We agreed to stick to a strict routine of three times a week, for forty-five minutes, straight after the school and nursery run. Working out together would be a good idea, we reckoned, because we'd be able to motivate and encourage each other. You're far less likely to put things off and make excuses when you've got a gym buddy.

The instructor taught us how to use the variety of weight training machines, like pull-downs and leg presses, initially beginning at a low resistance level and building things up progressively. I really liked working with weights, as opposed to cardio machines like treadmills and exercise bikes. While you don't always break a sweat with weights, you'll burn calories, you'll improve your strength, and the following day you have that telltale ache that suggests you've toned all the right muscles. But I fully admit, after the first couple of sessions I felt like I'd been hit by a ten-ton truck.

'I can't do this . . . I can't go back . . .' I remember telling Tyson, as I soothed my aching limbs.

'Stick with it, Paris,' he said. 'A sound body is a sound mind.'

No one knows more about the all-round benefits of fitness training than my husband. To him, exercise is the key to life. That release of endorphins – the so-called 'happy hormones' – keeps him positive and keeps his low mood at bay. So, inspired by Tyson, I continued my gym habit. In fact, once I got into the swing of things it became quite addictive. Not only did I get a massive buzz from the training itself, I also felt a huge sense of satisfaction afterwards. As a mother, you're so used to thinking of others before yourself – it's instinctive, almost – but it felt so good to be getting out of the house and doing something for *me*, for once. I know three sessions per week isn't loads – some people can spend hours in the gym, like Tyson – but it made such a difference to my general well-being, and really set me up for the rest of the day. Having that headspace did me the world of good.

But, all that being said, I appreciate that going to the gym isn't an option for every parent. As well as the time and money elements, childcare can be an issue if there isn't an on-site crèche or if you don't have anyone to mind the kids. But there are, of course, alternative ways to keep fit and active. I've always been a big fan of brisk walking, for instance. If you can maintain a good pace for half an hour, and keep your breathing nice and steady, I think it's as good as any gym workout. Add a couple of hills or slopes into the mix (especially if you have a buggy to push) and you're entering serious calorie-burning, heart-pumping territory. I try to fit three or four walks into my weekly schedule, even if it's a few circuits of the local park. It's a great way to keep fit and, best of all, it doesn't cost a penny.

Walking is good for your state of mind, too. When Tyson went through his bad patch, there were days when I'd feel totally overwhelmed with anxiety. I had a husband who was drinking too much and having very dark thoughts, plus children who relied on me, and some-times I felt like my head was about to explode. But I found that leaving the house and pounding the pave-ments, either alone or with the kids, really helped to calm me down and clear my mind. I'd almost have to force myself out of the front door sometimes, especially if it was cold, wet and blowing a gale. Staying at home and watching *Loose Women* with a cup of coffee often felt like the preferable option.

'Get your raincoat on, Paris, and get some fresh air,' I'd say, trying to drum up some enthusiasm. 'No excuses. You know you'll feel better afterwards.'

More often than not I'd stroll along the promenade in Morecambe, collecting my thoughts while Little Tyson snoozed in his pushchair. Even little things like treating myself to an ice cream, watching the seagulls hopping about or chatting to a couple of elderly tourists would be enough to lift my spirits. I'd always return home in a much better frame of mind. Walking helped me cope with life's challenges back then, and it still does to this day. If in doubt, get yourself out.

* * *

While I try to maintain a healthy weight (I've always hovered around the size 10 mark) it's something I've never obsessed over. I don't own a set of scales, for instance, because, like many women, my body weight naturally yo-yos, and fluctuates from day to day or week to week, and numbers on a display can often be deceptive. I much prefer to gauge any gains or losses by the way my clothes fit. I'll know it's time to rein in my crisps and chocolate habit when my skinny jeans start to feel a bit more snug than usual.

But I do think that my metabolism – the rate at which I burn calories – has begun to slow down a little. It's probably an age thing. In my teens and twenties, I could eat whatever I wanted without gaining a single ounce. But when I hit my thirties, if I overindulged – too much pizza and pasta while on holiday, perhaps – I'd feel my waistband tightening as a result. I also found it much harder to lose the extra 'baby weight' after giving birth to Adonis and Athena.

Most people will agree that a sensible combination of diet and exercise is the best way to manage your weight. 'Eat less, move more,' we're often told by health professionals (a message echoed by Tyson, who's something of an authority on this matter). With my gym sessions, my power-walking and my hectic lifestyle, I think I do all right with the exercise bit. As for the diet ... well, let's say that's a harder nut to crack. Because when it comes to eating, I've always had a hearty appetite. I just love my food. I'm not the sort of person who'll nibble a couple of lettuce leaves before announcing they're full, or who'll order a starter instead of a main. I'm a proper three-course-meal-plus-coffee type of girl. A large, tasty plateful of food is one of my great pleasures in life, especially when someone else is cooking. Dining with Tyson at a posh Manchester restaurant is my idea of heaven, and I'm very partial to our weekend takeaways with the family, too.

But if I have a food weakness, it's my late-night snacking. Some people do wine o'clock . . . I do crisps o'clock. When the kids are in bed and the chores are all done, I'll curl up on the couch with a grab-bag of Sweet Chilli Walker's Sensations. They're just so moreish. I know it's not good for me – a dietician would no doubt tell me to opt for a banana or some nuts – but I suppose it's my little treat to myself. After a tough day with the kids, I feel the need to indulge in a bit of comfort eating, and I won't let myself feel too guilty about it. Much worse, I reckon, is my awful habit of picking at the children's leftovers, if I've made them a quick tea. I'm sure I'm not alone in this, but I'll often find myself absent-mindedly grazing on their curly fries and chicken nuggets. I'm like a human dustbin. I can't help myself.

So whenever I feel the need to lose a bit of weight, in the first instance I'll summon up some willpower and try to cut down the snack-nibbling and the leftovers-nicking. If that doesn't work, I might consider a more structured healthy-eating regime. In the past I've tried a couple of very well-known weight loss programmes – the type that rightly promote healthy eating and balanced diets – and have shed a few pounds in the process. I'm not a fan of crash diets or detox plans; I hate the idea of starving or depriving myself of food. I'd feel so miserable with an empty, grumbling stomach that I'd probably reach straight for the snacks and end up piling my weight back on. And that would totally defeat the whole object.

So, rather than taking extreme, quick-fix measures, I much prefer to opt for the sensible, gradual option. This way, I don't need to cut the portion size – I can still enjoy a nice big plateful – but I just tweak the ingredients and reduce the calories. So that might mean less red meat and carbohydrates (not easy for me, as I'm a sucker for pasta and potatoes) in favour of lean poultry and fresh vegetables. I only like eating veg that's been cooked through, however, such as roasted carrots or steamed cabbage. I'm not really sure why, but there's something about raw salad ingredients like lettuce, cucumber and coleslaw that turns my stomach.

This type of meal can easily fit in with my busy lifestyle, too. Many of the recipes, like spaghetti Bolognese or shepherd's pie, are filling and nutritious enough to be suitable for the whole family. When it comes to having sweet treats, the cakes and puddings we might enjoy at weekends can easily be replaced with yoghurts and fruit salads.

As for drinks, if I'm on a health kick I'll tend to stick to water during the day – tap or bottled – and will try to limit my tea and coffee intake (too much caffeine makes me feel a bit wired and spaced out). If I'm going out for the evening, and sticking to soft drinks, I'll choose a Coke Zero (I find Diet Coke too gassy) or, if I fancy something stronger, I'll grab myself a rosé spritzer or a fancy cocktail. I rarely drink alcohol – I can have a perfectly fun time when I'm sober – but when I do, I like it sweet and fruity, so it tastes like fizzy pop. I'm not really into extra-dry wines or champagnes, and much prefer a nice piña colada or strawberry daiquiri, especially when I'm on holiday or on a girls' night out.

'Everything in moderation' is a motto of mine. I never drink to get drunk. I like to stay in control of my actions and can't bear the thought of having a hangover the following day, and being unable to do my jobs or look after the children. I've also seen the terrible effect that alcohol misuse can have on people – it almost ruined Tyson's life, before he managed to mend his ways – and that's enough to put me off. I hope I'm setting a good example to my kids, too, because I'd hate them to go through what their dad did. If they do choose to drink alcohol when they're older, I just hope they do so sensibly.

* * *

I'm touching wood as I write this, but I'm very lucky to enjoy good health. Other than a few pregnancy-related issues and incidents, I've never needed to go to hospital and, on a day-to-day basis, seldom suffer with illnesses other than the usual coughs, colds and sore throats. When I visit my local GP surgery, it's more often than not for a consultation regarding one of the children. Once they start going to school, picking up all sorts of germs and bugs becomes an inevitability.

On the rare occasions I do feel under the weather, I have to be extremely unwell before I send myself to bed. With all the kids to look after, it's a last resort for me. Fortunately, I can always rely on my mam to take over the childcare reins if necessary – she'll travel up to Morecambe at the drop of a hat – and Tyson, Venezuela and Prince will also do their bit to muck in. This was what had to happen just before Christmas 2022. I was struck down with horrendous back pain. I think I'd jarred something during a gym session – maybe I overdid it on one of the machines – and a dull ache lingered for a couple of days.

Then, as I was getting out of bed one morning, my back totally locked and seized up. The pain was so agonising I could hardly move. That day I was due to travel to London with Tyson – I'd planned to do some shopping while he was attending a business meeting – but I had to bail out at the last minute. Luckily my mam was staying with us at the time, so she helped get the kids dressed and fed, and my friends Shannon and Cathy did the morning school run.

Later that day the pain became so excruciating I had no option but to call 999. Four paramedics soon arrived, giving me gas and air to ease the pain and trying unsuccessfully to get me out of bed. Transferring me to hospital wouldn't be possible, they said, so they organised for a GP to prescribe me medication to take at home.

I was diagnosed with sciatica – a pressured nerve – and was advised to have total bed rest until everything calmed down. Tyson returned from London the following day and helped out with the kids, alongside Mam. For forty-eight hours I was pretty much out for the count. All I did was sleep. After three days, things began to ease, thank goodness, and I was eventually able to get out of bed and move around. But I had to take it easy for a couple of weeks afterwards; I avoided carrying the kids wherever possible and did the household chores at half-pace. Although my back problem was awful at the time, I'm very much hoping it was a one-off.

* * *

I'm fortunate to enjoy pretty robust mental health. I'm forever grateful to have been born with a sunny nature, and to be generally quite a positive and optimistic person. Don't get me wrong, there have been times when I've felt totally down in the dumps – family life can feel overwhelming – but I've never experienced the black cloud of depression. Being married to a sufferer, you learn to see the signs – the despair, the numbness, the hopelessness – and that's never something I've recognised in myself.

Like most parents, every now and then I'll have the day from hell, when nothing seems to go to plan, everything seems to pile up, and you go to bed feeling like you're a failure, and the worst wife and mother in the world. I've had some mornings when I've come home from a school run and dissolved into tears, due to the stress and strain of getting a bunch of bolshie, boisterous kids out of the house. But it's in those moments, when I'm feeling a little sorry for myself, that I'll take a break and have a breather. I might grab a glass of water and sit down with a magazine for ten minutes, or I might ring my mam or my sister for a quick chat; anything to help me calm down and chill out. And then I'll get my act together and put my best foot forward.

You've got this, Paris, I'll say to myself, as I start work on decluttering the kitchen. *Dig deep and crack on . . .*

Simply being around other people can give me a lift too, whether that's walking over to a friend's for a cake and a cuppa or just getting out of the car and chatting to the other mams at the school gates. Parenting can be a lonely experience – especially if you're a first-time mother, or have just moved to a new area – and interacting with others can snap you out of that isolation. I've been there. In the early days of Tyson's career, we went to live in Holland for a few months to be near his training camp, where he spent most of his waking hours. Venezuela and Prince were only toddlers, and during the day I used to feel really glum and gloomy; our house was in the middle of nowhere, so it was quite hard to meet other people and make new friends. One morning, I dragged the three of us out for a walk to a nearby village – the kids had been driving me mad – and just happened to hear an English accent in the local shop.

'Oh my God, you're from *England* . . .' I said, charging over to a very startled-looking elderly tourist. I then nattered to him non-stop for twenty minutes, about

211

anything and everything. No doubt I bored him to death, but he was very sweet with me. I walked back home with a real spring in my step. That brief encounter and that human interaction had made my day.

A traditional girls' night out is another great escape route for me. I really look forward to getting dressed up and having a catch-up with my female pals, who I meet every fortnight or so for a meal or a few drinks, usually in Morecambe or Lancaster. Our main objective is to have a giggle and a gossip – as busy parents, we treasure our precious downtime – but we'll also chat about our kids and our partners, offering each other advice, encouragement and solidarity if need be.

Sometimes you might want to share some good news (another baby on the way, perhaps?) or other times you might need a shoulder to cry on. Either way, it's always great to speak freely and openly, with a group of people you can trust. Women supporting women can be such a powerful thing. I only wish I'd opened up to my friends when I was going through all the trauma with Tyson. At the time, I didn't want to bother them with my problems. I've since learned my lesson, though. I don't bottle things up any more. It's always good to talk.

* * *

'Keep yourself tidy' is a motto my mam lives by. 'When you look good, you feel good, and when you look rubbish, you feel rubbish,' she'll say, and I couldn't agree more. Dressing nicely always improves my mood, whether it's the clean and comfy tracksuit I'll wear while I'm doing my chores, or the smart jeans and jacket I'll change into if I'm lunching with Tyson. For me, it's about presenting myself in the best way I can, for my own self-respect more than anything. If I was to roll out of bed and put on clothes that were grubby or scruffy I'd feel totally out of sorts, like I was letting my standards slip. It's just the way I've been brought up. The Gypsy community at Tilts Farm prided itself in keeping up appearances, whether it was your sparkling-clean trailer or your beautifully dressed children. Even now, I won't let my sons out of the house if their hair isn't styled and gelled. I once posted a family photo on Instagram – I think it was Athena's christening – and somebody commented that my boys looked 'like 1950s mobsters'. Well, I'd rather that than looking like scruff-bags . . .

Taking pride in your appearance shouldn't depend on being conventionally slim or attractive, though, despite what some women's magazines might imply. I reckon you can make the best of yourself whatever your shape or size. Take my mother, for instance. She's an extremely good-looking woman who is always fabulously turned out, from her elegant clothes and accessories to her stylish hair and make-up. Friends and family will often shower her with compliments ('Wow, looking good, Lynda . . .'), which, as you'd imagine, is music to her ears.

The fact my mam is a plus-size woman is an irrelevance to her. She never moans about her weight, and doesn't use it as an excuse not to look her best. Instead, she carefully chooses outfits that complement her body shape and that make her feel comfortable: a nice pair of heels, a fitted trouser suit and a matching clutch bag, perhaps. Mam is incredibly happy in her skin. She isn't remotely vain or full of herself, she's just one of the most body-confident people I know, and I can't help but be inspired by that. Whenever I'm asked who my style guru is, I'll often say 'My mam.'

Like her, I only feel at my best when I'm looking smart and tidy. My life somehow feels less chaotic and more disciplined if I'm dressed up rather than dressed down. I've also taken her advice about not following trends and fashions, and dressing for myself, not for others. I generally choose clothes that suit my figure, accentuating the bits I like and covering the bits I don't. This is certainly the case when I'm choosing a fancy outfit for a big title fight, when – as Mrs Tyson Fury – I know I'll attract a lot of attention. I tend to opt for a vibrantly coloured dress, short or long – perhaps with a few sequins or feathers for some added glitz – which I'll team with matching shoes and handbag. The outfit has to be practical and comfortable as well, something I can easily jump up and down in (which I often do at ringside). I've worn designer gowns to fights, and I've also worn high street off-the-peg numbers. Either's fine to me, as long as my dress looks good and feels great.

I have my body flaws and imperfections – don't we all? – but, from a young age, Mam taught me not to become fixated on them.

'Aw, it looks too tight,' I used to say when I was a teenager, scrutinising a new outfit in front of the mirror.

'Don't be so picky, Paris,' she'd say. 'You're young, you're healthy. Be thankful for what you've got.'

Making the best of ourselves is a family trait, I'd say. Most of my female relatives – on my mam's side and my dad's – push the boat out to look decent. Even my Granny Mary keeps the glamour stakes high, regardless of being a housebound 91-year-old. Her nightdresses and dressing gowns are immaculate – she looks like a Hollywood film star – and, with the help of her carer, she still faces the day with her make-up on, her hair done and a spritz of her favourite perfume. What a legend.

It was Granny who taught me how to look after my skin properly. I have the most straightforward beauty routine you could imagine, perhaps not what you'd expect from a qualified beauty therapist. Each morning and evening I cleanse my face with mild soap and water, or a gentle facial wash. I then moisturise with a face cream suitable for sensitive skin, since I'm prone to eczema. It doesn't have to be fancy – I rarely spend more than a tenner – and I'll regularly chop and change products, often opting for own brands from high street beauty stores. And I try not to totally smother my face with cream; I use it quite sparingly, so I can give my skin a chance to breathe. I generally steer clear of toners, exfoliators and face masks, too, because they tend to irritate my skin. And that's basically the long and short of my beauty routine, as advised by Granny (whose skin is still amazingly smooth, by the way). Told you it was simple!

I have a similar no-nonsense approach to haircare. I'm lucky to be blessed with a thick and healthy head of hair – enough for two people, I was once told by a stylist – and you might say it's my crowning glory. Other women often ask how I look after it, and are often surprised how ordinary my routine is. I have it cut three times a year, and get it coloured every six weeks or so (I'm naturally blond, but just have it lightened) and I never spend daft money on expensive shampoos and conditioners; I just grab whatever's on offer in the supermarket. And if I'm ever attending a special occasion – a party, or a title fight – I'll always style my own hair. No one can manage my crazy mane better than me – there's a reason why some friends call me the 'Lion King'.

As for make-up, I have my two 'faces': my day-to-day face and my going-out face. On a normal morning, I sport the natural look, just dabbing on some blusher and lip gloss, together with some mascara (it literally takes me two minutes to do). In summer, I might apply some fake tan on a Sunday night, just to give me a nice, sun-kissed glow that lasts me the week.

In the evening, if I'm socialising, I'll apply a thin layer of foundation – I don't like trowelling it on – as well as my favourite lipstick and eyeshadow. For some extra glitz 'n' glam, I might apply some false eyelashes, but that's only if I have the time. More often than not I'm in a hurry to get out – I've invariably been waylaid by the kids – and I'll end up having to apply my make-up on the go, in the kitchen, almost as I'm heading out of the door. I've also been known to do my face while I'm making dinner, holding a wooden spoon in one hand and a mascara wand with the other. It always makes me smile when people on social media see a photo of me all dolled up, and ask me who's done my make-up, perhaps imagining I have a personal beautician to hand. I think they're quite surprised when I tell them it's a DIY job.

Now she's a teenager, my eldest daughter Venezuela has entered the world of make-up. She's allowed to wear it during the day as long as she keeps it light and subtle. I'm less strict if she's going to a birthday party – like many young girls, she loves dressing up – but if I think she's overdone it with the brows or the contouring I'll let her know.

'Tone down that foundation, Venezuela, you look like a chequerboard,' I'll say.

'Aw, Mam, do I have to?' she'll moan, before doing as she's told. Sometimes, Mam knows best.

I rarely visit a beauty salon these days. I used to enjoy the occasional treatment in years gone by – a gentle facial, or a relaxing massage – but I have neither the time nor the inclination any more. It's just not top of the list of my priorities at the moment. I get my nails done regularly at a local place – I'm a serial nail-biter, unfortunately – but that's more of a chore than a treat. In truth, I really don't have much pampering in my life, other than the occasional spa day with my girlfriends (and even that's only a couple of times a year, at most). But I'm really not complaining. There are other ways that I can relax and chill out. An afternoon nap or a coffee in town is more than enough for me. Even better, a holiday abroad with the family (especially when Tyson takes the kids off my hands for a couple of hours).

So my message to other mams out there is this: give yourselves a break. Look after your well-being, do whatever makes you feel good and don't feel guilty about prioritising your own needs. Never look at me-time as a luxury – look at it as a necessity and realise that it's the sensible thing to do, not the selfish thing to do. Because caring for yourself means you can better care for others. A happier you equals a happier family.

CHAPTER NINE

FOR BETTER, FOR WORSE

OTHER THAN HAVING my beautiful children, marrying Tyson is the best thing that's ever happened to me. I'm so happy and proud to be his wife – he's an amazing person, and a fantastic father – and I think he and I make a pretty good team. I can't believe we'll soon be celebrating our fifteenth wedding anniversary – what a crazy rollercoaster ride that's been! – but I can safely say that, even after all these years, I love Tyson more than ever. Despite facing the occasional hiccup and hurdle (we have our highs and lows, like most married couples), I feel truly blessed to have him by my side as we navigate family life together.

Sadly, in the world of sport and showbiz, you hear of many high-profile celebrity marriages that break up. Some couples can't cope with the pressure of life in the limelight – especially if fame hits them suddenly or unexpectedly – and they unfortunately don't last the distance. There have been times in our marriage when we might have gone the same way, but I'm so pleased we've managed to work through our problems. Being together for such a long time has definitely played to our advantage. When we first started dating as teenagers, Tyson wasn't remotely famous – he was an ambitious amateur boxer, working his way up the sporting ladder – and we hardly had two pennies to rub together. He could barely afford to fill his car up with petrol when he visited me in Doncaster, and we had our date nights in the less expensive restaurant chains. I was drawn to his big heart, not his bank balance, and I definitely married him for all the right reasons.

Neither of us had a clue that Tyson was going to hit the big time like he did, but when he shot to global stardom we'd already built the foundations of our relationship. Our bond was strong and solid enough to cope with this newfound fame. After Tyson's victory our lives changed overnight – people recognised us wherever we went, which took some getting used to – but, away from the spotlight, we were still Tyson and Paris, childhood sweethearts, who shopped in Asda and did the school run. And that remains the case to this day. But fame has put different pressures on us and, while my husband may be the star of the show, I like to think I've played an important supporting role. During his boxing career I've

been on hand to talk things through, to calm his nerves
and to boost his morale. I like to think I'm the anchor
that keeps him steady and the linchpin that prevents his
wheels falling off. The wind beneath his wings.

So what's the secret of our success? This may sound
obvious but, first and foremost, we genuinely care for
one another. I'd do anything for Tyson – I'm there for
him whenever he needs my love and support – and I
know he feels the same about me. When he's feeling
down, I'll lift him up. When I'm super-busy, he'll help me
out. Equally importantly, we're also the very best of
friends. When we're in each other's company we can be
ourselves, and we feel so content and comfortable
together. No one knows me better than Tyson. He can
take one look at me, or hear the tone of my voice, and
know exactly what kind of mood I'm in: good, bad or
somewhere in between.

All good relationships also need an element of
romance, of course – it helps if you still fancy your other
half! – but I think friendship and companionship is just
as key. In other words, you need to *like* your partner as
well as *love* them. I've known couples who've sadly split
up because, once that first flush of love starts to fade –
which it inevitably does – they've realised they don't
actually have much in common, and aren't as well-suited
or as like-minded as they'd imagined. Tyson and I are

good pals as well as soulmates, and I hope this stands us in good stead for a long and happy marriage.

Sharing similar values and belief systems is crucial too, I believe, especially when it comes to family. As devoted parents, nothing matters more to us than our sons' and daughters' well-being. We're committed to bringing them up in a secure and stable home. To keep the household running smoothly, and the children well looked after, Tyson and I agree to work as a team and share the duties. It's only fair that we both do our bit and pull our weight. So I'll get up for the baby's night feed, perhaps, and he'll do the morning school and nursery run. Or, later in the day, I'll prepare our evening meal while Tyson tidies up the children's toys and games. At weekends, he might take the younger kids to see his family in Manchester, while I take the older kids on a shopping trip to the Trafford Centre (we'll all meet up later for a bite to eat). If he's away at training camp the burden falls on me, which can be exhausting, but I never feel resentful. My husband works very hard and sacrifices so much to provide for his family – boxing is a risky business – and my respect and admiration for him is endless.

But keeping your marriage on track isn't always easy, especially when family life is all-consuming. The pressures of raising children and running a household can drive a wedge between couples. You can end up running from one problem to another without pausing for breath or to wonder how each of you is coping. That's why Tyson and I work so hard to carve out time to talk, not just about the children, but about ourselves as well. That might mean arranging a date night – we try to eat out together every week, if we can – or sitting down on our own to talk through any problems. Emotional support is key to our partnership, and we've often had to draw upon each other's strength and positivity. Over the years we've experienced the good times and the bad, from the triumphs of my husband's title fights to the traumas of our children's health scares. We've shared and survived.

But one of the very low points came in our own relationship, six or seven years ago. We were in danger of collapsing when Tyson's mental health spiralled and he went totally off the rails, with lots of heavy drinking and (to my horror) reckless drug-taking. I seriously considered leaving him at one point, as his wild behaviour was making me utterly miserable. But instead I gritted my teeth and persevered, because this wasn't the Tyson I knew and loved, and I reckoned our marriage was worth saving. For the sake of our family and our future, Tyson eventually found the strength to fix his self-destructive behaviour and worked hard to manage his depression.

Coming through it has only strengthened us. Now it's me and Tyson against the world.

* * *

When I was a young girl, I dreamed of meeting my own Prince Charming. I imagined a fairy-tale wedding, raising lots of kids and living happily ever after. Tyson arrived on the scene and he was just the tall, handsome stranger I'd always visualised. I was only sixteen when I began dating him – we met at a wedding reception in Nottingham – and he became my first and only boyfriend. I was the happiest girl in the world when he proposed to me just a couple of months later, although we didn't get officially engaged for another couple of years, when I was eighteen. Not that our engagement went totally smoothly. A series of blazing rows culminated in a brief separation – this included a tiff about Tyson wanting to change our wedding date – and at one point it looked like our courtship was over. But Tyson and I couldn't bear to be apart – we just knew we were perfect for each other – and we luckily managed to patch things up.

We were married in a Doncaster church, in November 2008, surrounded by close friends and family. As practising Christians, the religious ceremony and the exchanging of vows meant a great deal to us. Fifteen years later, we still hold fast to those solemn commitments. Tyson and I firmly believe that we are life partners, for better or for worse, in sickness and in health, till death us do part. To us, tying the knot is more than just a piece of paper and a pile of presents. Marriage is one of life's great gifts, something that should be cherished and celebrated. But I appreciate not everybody has our luck, and that things don't always work out for others. My family were thrilled to bits when they met Tyson. They admired his kind and caring nature – they knew he'd look after their precious daughter – and were impressed with his sporting ambitions (back then, he was fighting on the amateur circuit). My Granny Mary was especially pleased, since she'd always told me to aim high when it came to choosing a boyfriend. Never mincing her words, she'd say to me in her American drawl:

'Look for browner nuts in higher bushes, Paris, because you can pick up shit anywhere.'

It's a saying that still makes me laugh.

Of course when Tyson and I first got together, everything seemed so fresh and exciting. My heart missed a beat whenever he entered the room, and neither of us could bear to be apart from one another. But, as our marriage evolved and familiarity grew, those crazy-in-love feelings naturally began to fade. Our fondness for each other didn't dwindle, it simply became different; more settled and comforting, perhaps.

You have to work harder to keep the romance alive, and I know that's easier said than done when both partners have busy schedules, and especially when you have lots of children sapping your time and energy. It's so easy to get stuck in a rut; you find yourself in a Groundhog Day routine of school runs and house jobs, followed by dinnertime, bathtime and bedtime. But with a little bit of effort and invention (on both sides) you can rekindle that spark, just like the good old days.

With that in mind, Tyson and I try to have some time alone at least once or twice a week, whether it's grabbing lunch in Morecambe or going for a walk in the countryside. Tyson's spontaneous nature can sometimes be an issue for me, though. I can be up to my neck in housework – cleaning the fridge out, for instance – and my husband will bound into the kitchen, suggesting we go into Morecambe for coffee and cake and expecting me to drop everything straight away. Usually, as is often the case with us, we'll reach some sort of compromise. I'll ask him to hang fire for half an hour, giving me time to finish the job and have a quick change of outfit before we head into town.

If we're in the mood for an evening out, we might arrange a date night in Manchester, perhaps a trip to the cinema followed by a meal in our favourite Italian restaurant. Our babysitter Gabby will often look after the children, or my mam if she's staying with us.

'I feel like I've hardly seen you all week,' Tyson will say if we've been like ships in the night. 'Let's go for a nice meal, just you and me . . .'

'Ooh, that'd be lovely,' I'll reply, ready for a break from the daily grind.

When you're caught up in the whirlwind of family life, it can be easy to take each other for granted. Sometimes you need to remind yourselves why you started dating in the first place, and what sparked that initial attraction. Quality time together is really important, and a change of scenery can make all the difference.

I love getting dressed up for a date night. Looking smart and chic makes me feel good – especially if I've spent most of the week doing the chores in my tracksuit – but I like to glam up for my husband, too. I will choose a favourite outfit from my dressing room before applying my make-up, styling my hair and dabbing on some perfume. Tyson likes getting spruced up, too. He always looks immaculate when we're out together, from his neatly trimmed beard to his freshly shined shoes.

Making the effort for each other is incredibly important, I think. My mother often warned me against letting my standards slip, appearance-wise. She'd seen other women becoming a bit slapdash, and their marriages faltering as a result, and she was determined not to fall into that trap herself. Mam never, ever looked scruffy, even when she was cleaning the house. In the early days of our marriage, she'd often pass on her good old-fash-ioned values.

'You've got a man, Paris . . . now keep him,' she'd say. 'Always look nice and smart. Show him you're interested. Don't let him think you're not bothered.'

While I happen to agree with her, this can't be one-sided. There has to be respect between both parties. A husband should want to look his best for his wife, and vice versa.

Whenever we enjoy a romantic meal for two, Tyson and I try to avoid discussing the kids. We love them to bits, of course, but they do tend to dominate our conver-sation back home ('Guess how many nappies the baby filled today, Tyson?'), so, for a change, we'll linger long over our meal and talk about other topics. We might chat about each other's business interests, perhaps – like my latest Instagram promotion, or Tyson's upcoming boxing schedule – or we might discuss a story that's hit the news headlines.

Occasionally we'll natter about our future plans, and might kick around ideas about holiday destinations or house renovations. Tyson and I never get the chance to chat like this when we're surrounded by children. Going out for a family meal isn't the most relaxing experience in the world. So it's really refreshing to be able to sit in a quiet restaurant, just the two of us, without having to wipe Adonis' face or cut up Athena's chicken. And it's great for me to finally sit back, relax, and allow someone else to do the cooking.

There are other ways to keep the romance alive in a relationship, too. The smallest gesture can make all the difference. Tyson will sometimes surprise me with a bunch of flowers or a box of chocolates – both put a massive smile on my face – and, very occasionally (and to really pull on my heartstrings), he'll dig out the pink memory box that contains mementos from our court-ship. Among many items, it includes a cinema ticket for *King Kong* (our first date!), a plastic pretend engagement ring and a handwritten love note from Tyson.

'In short, I will part with anything for you,' it reads. 'There is only one happiness in life; to love, and to be loved.' Those words really strike a chord with me, and always make me feel quite emotional.

Tyson can be really tender and thoughtful when he wants to be. He's got quite a sentimental streak. Out of the blue, he'll text me an old photograph of the pair of us at a post-fight party, perhaps something he's found while scrolling online. Occasionally, he'll tag it with a message telling me how beautiful I looked that night, and how happy that memory makes him feel. In interviews, he often speaks quite openly about our relationship and isn't shy to admit how much he loves me, and how much he relies on his 'rock', as he calls me. I'm proud that Tyson is the first to say that men shouldn't feel afraid to express their feelings in this way, and that it's a perfectly healthy thing to do.

Tyson is quite tactile too, and has no qualms about public displays of affection, whether that's giving me a peck on the cheek or a bear hug (being so huge, he gives the *best* cuddles in the world). I'm quite demonstrative myself, and love that feeling of closeness. The pair of us will often hold hands or link arms as we're walking down the street, which could probably be seen as cute or cringe, depending on your point of view. Our kids don't seem to mind at all, though. I think they like seeing Mam and Dad happy with life and happy with each other.

But, while I consider myself a very warm-hearted person, I wouldn't describe myself as a big romantic. In all honesty – and forgive me for sounding old-fashioned here – I think this is the man's department. Of course I'm always on hand to offer Tyson all the practical support and TLC he needs (and he's required plenty in the past), but I don't really do spontaneous romantic gestures and present-buying, other than for birthdays and at Christmas. But, then again, I don't think Tyson expects me to. He likes being the man who bears gifts, and likes coming home with surprises. These little treats are a token of his appreciation, I suppose; a way of saying thank you for being there for him and the children. This means a lot to me. Who doesn't like feeling valued?

*   *   *

Sometimes I find the best way to freshen up our relationship is with a short break or a weekend away together. This doesn't happen as often as we'd like – Tyson's schedule can be so crazy – but, two or three times a year, we'll manage to sort out the childcare (thanks, Mam!) and escape somewhere for a few days. Often I'll piggyback onto one of my husband's business trips, effectively killing two birds with one stone. A few years ago, Tyson had to fly to Prague to attend a promotional event, and he suggested we turned it into a much-needed mini-break.

We had such a wonderful time there – Prague is one of the most beautiful cities in Europe – and we savoured every minute of our quality time together. We stayed in a fabulous hotel, dined in some lovely restaurants and explored the Old Town, visiting historical landmarks like Prague Castle and having romantic strolls along Charles Bridge. We were properly loved up. It really was like

233

being a young engaged couple again. Even the inevitable selfie-seekers and autograph hunters couldn't dampen anything; I've just had to accept that Tyson is one of the most recognisable sportsmen in the world (you really can't mistake him) and that he'll attract attention wherever we go.

New York City proved to be another memorable mini-break, back in 2021. It was short and sweet but totally epic. Tyson and I had made a diversion from a family holiday in Florida, since Mam had come with us and was happy to look after the children for a night. It was all very last-minute, which made it all the more exciting. We flew up to JFK airport and, after Tyson's daytime meeting, made the most of our impromptu trip. We don't really drink much, as a rule – Tyson only has a couple of beers now and again – but, that evening, we indulged in a few cocktails and ended up getting quite tipsy. I can still picture ourselves cuddled up in a horse-drawn carriage taking us around Central Park, singing our hearts out ('American Pie' probably) and crying with laughter. We were both bursting with happiness. Life's all about creating memories, I believe, and this remains one of my favourites.

Me and Tyson also went for a shopping spree at Bergdorf Goodman, one of Manhattan's big department stores.

'Get anything you want, Paris,' said Tyson – maybe it was the drink speaking – so I did. I woke up the next morning in our swanky hotel, with a rare hangover, surrounded by a pile of Bergdorf Goodman bags, unable to remember what I'd bought. *What the heck is in those bags?* I thought to myself, fearing a few regret-buys. Luckily I'd chosen pretty well. I just had to figure out a way of squeezing my brand new clothes and accessories into my suitcase back in Florida.

We've been lucky to have a few short sunshine breaks, too, usually in the wake of a family holiday. After a fortnight chasing after the kids in 90-degree heat, Tyson and I are often ready for some serious chillaxing, by ourselves. We've enjoyed a couple of Mediterranean cruises, one around Spain, the other around the Greek islands. We had a blast on both occasions. Not only was it lovely to get the chance to unwind together, and enjoy some peace and quiet, we could rest easy in the knowledge that the children were being well looked after by their granny at home. And, thanks to modern technology there are ways of keeping in touch, so a nightly video call allowed us to hook up with the Morecambe posse every night.

One of our most meaningful getaways was a six-week stint on the Costa del Sol, in the winter of 2017. Tyson was planning a boxing comeback following his long period of depression and his trainer, Ben, thought it would be a good idea to decamp to Marbella for a while. It would be a good opportunity for Tyson to get his mind and body in shape, well away from the media spotlight. We took the whole family with us (Valencia was only a few weeks old) and our long-time friends Dave and Cathy also came along to keep us company.

Our pals were happy to babysit, too, which meant that Tyson and I were able to have the occasional night out, just by ourselves. So we'd get dressed up, drive over to the port area of the city and have a quiet meal in a little bistro, where we'd have a nice relaxed chat and watch the world go by. The previous two years had been dreadful – Tyson's mood swings and wild behaviour had definitely come between us – and we almost had to rebuild our relationship. This trip to Marbella, far away from the pressures of home, really helped with the healing process. It felt like we'd jumped off the world for a few weeks. By the time we returned to Morecambe – a little reluctantly, if truth be told – our flame had been rekindled.

Tyson's boxing schedule has also taken me to the United States on many occasions. I've watched him fight in New York, Los Angeles and Las Vegas, although I wouldn't exactly call them holidays or restful breaks. I spend half the time stressed to the eyeballs, worrying that my husband is going to get through the fight unscathed and constantly checking the children are OK at home (again, my beloved mam will hold the fort ... what would I do without her?). I tend to get to the venue city a few days before, which gives me time to hook up with Tyson, albeit briefly, in the middle of the crazy run-up. It's always fabulous to see him – by then, we'll have been separated for six weeks or so – and the first thing we do is go for a lovely meal in a luxury hotel, just the two of us. Being apart from Tyson makes me realise how much I miss him and crave him, and makes me much less likely to take him for granted. Absence really does make the heart grow fonder. Tyson and I are often in tears when we first clap eyes on each other at the airport, like a pair of lovesick teenagers.

Watching the big fight itself, usually flanked by my brothers-in-law, Shane and Hughie, is invariably a nerve-wracking experience. I endure it rather than enjoy it. Seeing your soulmate getting punched in the face is just horrendous, even if he's cruising towards victory, and I'm the happiest woman in the stadium when the contest ends. The relief I feel is incredible, something that's quite obvious if you see any post-fight footage of me and Tyson. He knows how much trauma I go through – he says he can hear me yelling and screaming throughout the bout – and he can't wait to give me a hug and a kiss once I've clambered into the boxing ring.

He's even been known to grab the microphone and serenade me. In 2015, over in Düsseldorf, he sang Aerosmith's 'Don't Want to Miss a Thing' after beating Wladimir Klitschko and, at that moment in time, it felt like we were the only two people in the arena. On the eve of the fight I'd told Tyson I was pregnant with our third child, so our emotions were already running high. It was such a romantic gesture, a genuine declaration of love, that happened to be witnessed by millions of viewers around the world.

*   *   *

But let me be honest here. Like all marriages, our life together isn't always rosy and romantic. While it's never easy to be apart from Tyson for long periods of time, it's just as hard to have him at home seven days a week. This is especially the case if there isn't a fight on the horizon, when he has much more spare time on his hands. He always does some kind of training in the morning – a gym workout, or a run along the beach – but I'll often find him hanging around the house afterwards, getting under my feet. I run my home like a well-oiled machine – doing the chores, changing the babies, cooking the meals – but when Tyson's around he puts a big spanner in the works. In the aftermath of a big fight, he likes to think he can just waltz back into the house and not worry that it mucks up my routine. This can be incredibly irritating. Every time I move a muscle he'll ask where I'm going, or what am I doing, or whether he can come too.

'Forget all that washing, Paris, let's go out for lunch,' he'll say as I'm knee-deep in family laundry. 'We can go to that nice pub you like, and maybe have a walk afterwards.'

'No chance, Tyson,' I'll reply. 'I need to get this done and dusted. It's full of school uniforms and PE kits that the kids need tomorrow. We can do lunch on Friday.'

Then he'll go into a major sulk on the sofa for the rest of the afternoon, which actually is fine by me, because at least I know I'll get all my jobs done without interruption.

Tyson can become a lost soul when he's in between fights. He'll have gone from a tight, rigorous and disciplined daily routine to one workout per day. That lack of structure and motivation is really hard for him to handle – he misses the banter of his team and sparring partners, for sure – and he can get very edgy and restless. Other than helping me out with a few chores, like doing the school run, he finds it very hard to know how to fill his day. Unfortunately, he doesn't have strong interests outside of boxing – he's not really into golf, fishing or DIY, for instance – and, since he has a very short attention span, can get easily bored. And unlike me, he doesn't really enjoy spending time by himself – I'm totally fine with solitude but he much prefers to be surrounded by people. Perhaps that's another reason why we've had so many children, to keep Tyson company at all times!

Every day I thank God that Tyson's mental health is on an even keel right now but, knowing he's prone to emotional dips, I do worry how he'll cope with his eventual retirement. He'll have so much time on his hands then. I dearly hope he finds another vocation in life, whether or not it's connected with sport. I'm sure he'll settle on something else that will add new meaning and purpose to his life, although I doubt anything will ever come close to rivalling his boxing career. It's a subject we discuss a lot, when we sit down and chat over coffee.

It's always good to talk, as Tyson and I frequently remind each other. In the early days of our marriage, well before he was diagnosed with a mental health condition, we didn't communicate as well as we do now. Back then, he'd clam up whenever he experienced his low moods, and never wanted to talk about his feelings. From my standpoint, I just didn't understand why he was acting this way, and often felt quite shut out. I took it all quite personally – I'd get upset when he spent all day in bed, refusing point blank to engage with me – and I became quite annoyed and resentful.

It was only when Tyson was admitted to hospital in Lancashire, following a complete breakdown in 2016, that we fully realised the seriousness of his illness. It was such a frightening experience. Our friend Dave had been with Tyson at the time – he'd simply lost control of his body and mind, while trying to start his car – and he told me to get myself down to the hospital as soon as possible (luckily Shannon was on hand to mind the children). I arrived to find my husband in a very bad way. He was incredibly anxious and agitated, and it took a few hours for the medical team to calm him down. He spent half a day in hospital before being discharged, and was subsequently referred to a team of mental health specialists, who eventually diagnosed him with bipolar disorder and OCD. Receiving this clarity helped Tyson make sense of things and, in many ways, rescued our relationship. Not only did it explain Tyson's behaviour, particularly his severe mood swings, it also encouraged us to be more open and honest with each other.

Tyson still has occasional 'dips', which may be the case as long as he lives, but he's learning to manage and tolerate his condition. And with more insight into his mental health issues, I'm better able to cope, too. When I sense Tyson is starting to slump – he might become very quiet and withdrawn, with a telltale glazed expression – I'll allow him some space for a day or so. But if his low mood lingers we'll make time for a long chat, so he can unravel his thoughts and feelings. More often than not we'll come up with a strategy to brighten him up, which could be a long walk in the countryside to clear his head or a trip over to Manchester to see his family. I also monitor whether Tyson is getting enough sleep and keeping up his exercise, and isn't being tempted by the wrong kind of food or drink. With time and patience, his dark cloud usually passes.

'It's OK to not feel OK,' I'll say to him. 'Just be kind to yourself.'

'I will, Paris. I'll get through this.'

Tyson and I have learned to be good talkers, but that's not to say we don't have the occasional argument. I think tiffs and squabbles are perfectly normal in a marriage – wouldn't life be boring if we never disagreed? – and heated debate and discussion can often be beneficial, so long as it doesn't signify a deeper problem. This is my rule of thumb: if your relationship contains more good moments than bad, and more laughs than rows, then you're pretty much onto a winner.

These days, however, my husband and I tend to bicker more than quarrel. Our full-blown, plate-throwing, door-slamming arguments are long gone. In the early stages of our marriage we were extremely hot-headed, and the sparks would fly. We were very young, don't forget – I was only nineteen, Tyson a year my senior – and we'd never lived together before, so weren't used to each other's little habits and routines. Neither of us had realised how hard it was to share your life with another person, especially while cooped up in a 24-foot trailer. We rowed constantly – I remember once chasing him down the street, yelling various insults at him. Our life was one big soap opera.

But everything is much calmer in the Fury household nowadays. We've grown up and matured together, and have become far more tolerant and understanding of each other. We recognise the importance of compromise, too, and we make decisions between ourselves that are right for the family.

Like education, for example. When Venezuela left primary school, aged eleven, she made it clear she wanted to be home-schooled rather than attend the local secondary school. Tyson and I initially had a difference of opinion about this. He preferred the high school route for his daughter, whereas I wanted her to be educated at home while learning life skills, in keeping with our traditional Traveller ways. Luckily, Tyson and I were able to talk things through and we reached an agreement. For the last couple of years, Venezuela has studied a normal GCSE curriculum, with the help of a home tutor, and it's working out really well. Everybody's happy. Result.

Don't get me wrong, Tyson and I do lock horns now and again but it's usually about something relatively trivial, like when he puts out the wrong bins, or when I'm not as talkative as normal (often because I'm in tired-parent mode).

'What are you in a mood for?'

'I'm not in a mood, Tyson.'

'You hardly said two words at lunchtime.'

'I've been up all night with the baby and I'm exhausted, OK?'

But on the rare occasion that we do get very annoyed about something, we react in different ways. I yell and Tyson sulks. I do the shouting and he does the silences. I'm a bit like a volcano in that respect. When things get too much I'll have a major eruption – I'm sure the whole neighbourhood can hear me – but, once it's all out of my system, I'll soon be calm again and I'll move on. It's all very heat-of-the-moment stuff. Tyson, on the other hand, will stomp off in a huff and give me the silent treatment, sometimes for days on end, and will only speak to me via the kids: 'Ask your mam what we're having for tea,' and so on. I find this totally infuriating. I'd much rather get things out into the open and have a good blast, especially if we're arguing about something minor.

There have also been occasions, however, when Tyson and I have been in the middle of a tiff and have suddenly burst out laughing because one of us has put on a funny voice or pulled a stupid face. Luckily, we don't take ourselves too seriously – we definitely share the same daft sense of humour – and we have this ability to crack each other up. It's so important to have some fun in your relationship, I think, even if it means you acting like a couple of silly kids. Tyson and I can often be found dancing around the house together or having a singalong in the car at the top of our voices.

But having children around the place has definitely made us more aware of our general behaviour. Bickering and back-biting in front of the kids isn't a great look, and we try our best to avoid it. We don't always succeed – family life just doesn't work like that – but we prefer, if we can, to prevent any bad atmospheres. I want my children to be assured that their mam and dad have a very happy marriage, because it helps them feel safe and secure. A warring couple would have the opposite effect, I reckon. My parents, Jimmy and Lynda, had a rock-solid relationship – my siblings and I rarely saw them arguing – and I really benefited from a settled family life. Ideally, I'd like my own children to be brought up in a similar environment. The majority of kids crave stability and consistency in their lives.

I also believe that Tyson and I have a responsibility to be role models to our children. I want them to know what a strong, loving and respectful marriage looks like. I'm not saying we're a perfect couple by any means, but I think it's helpful for our kids to see their mother and father working as a team, sorting things out and supporting each other. They need to realise that good, healthy relationships require a great deal of compromise and cooperation. I dearly hope each of my children find their soulmate, like I did with Tyson, so they can settle down and raise a family of their own.

* * *

Being married to a world-famous celebrity has its advantages and disadvantages. Tyson's success in the boxing ring means I'm able to lead a very comfortable existence, and can enjoy the finer things in life. I've never hidden my fondness for designer gear and luxury holidays, and I'm grateful to live in a beautiful home and drive fabulous cars. Being financially secure also means our children are well provided for, although I'd prefer them not to rely on their dad's fame and fortune when they're adults, and instead to make their own mark as people, partners and parents. All that being said, money is certainly not the most important thing in my life. The health and welfare of my loved ones overrides everything, as far as I'm concerned. I'd rather live in a tent with a happy family than in a mansion with a sad one.

On the flip side, though, while we see ourselves as a normal couple (we try to stay as grounded as possible, the reason we've stayed put in Morecambe), Tyson and I have spent much of our marriage in the public eye. We appreciate that his high profile means that people are interested in what we do and where we go, as well as their fascination with our Gypsy heritage – but sometimes the attention can be a little hard to handle. The press might print false, far-fetched stories about me or Tyson, for example – though they've done that so often that I tend to turn a blind eye to tabloid gossip these days – or the paparazzi will stalk us whenever we're on holiday. We now have to resort to taking security with us, for the children's sake more than anything. That's a definite downside to our celebrity status – the lack of privacy can be frustrating – but we just have to accept it as part and parcel of life with Tyson. We just crack on with our usual routine as best we can.

This unwanted attention is one of the reasons we've agreed to take part in a couple of TV documentaries. By allowing cameras into the house, viewers around the world have been able to watch an honest and truthful portrayal of our family life that (we hope) has dispelled some of the claptrap they might have read in the newspapers. Importantly, it's also given Tyson a global platform to raise awareness about mental health, a subject that remains close to his heart. And we also like the idea of these documentaries acting as a permanent memorial of our family life; something that our kids, grandkids and great-grandkids could watch for years to come.

In some episodes, Tyson and I aren't always shown in the best light – there's plenty of footage of me looking worn out, and him having a strop – but that authenticity formed part of our terms and conditions. We only wanted to sign up for a documentary if it was a frank, warts-and-all representation of our family and our marriage. Any airbrushing or sugar-coating would just defeat the whole object, in our opinion, because we wanted viewers to see the real Tyson and Paris Fury. I'd often joke about our no-holds-barred, access-all-areas approach with the film crews.

'Come on in, team, welcome to the good, the bad and the ugly . . .' I'd say as I ushered them through our hallway each morning.

The feedback from our TV shows has been so positive, though. I think people now appreciate that Tyson and I are like most other thirty-something married couples with busy lives and crazy kids, experiencing the same ups and downs and twists and turns as everybody else.

But I also think it's plain to see how devoted we are to each other, and how strong we are together. I think the bond we have is very special. We may not be perfect, but we're perfect for each other.

It's true to say that marriage has taught us a great deal about ourselves over the last fifteen years. It's shown us how tackling life's challenges is so much easier when you have a soulmate by your side, offering you love and support when you need it most. A person who can wipe away your tears when times are bad, and share in your joy when times are good. Someone with whom you can create happy memories, and make future plans. I'm glad to say that married life right now is fabulous. Team Fury is in great shape. And I'm so excited to discover what lies in store for us.

Chapter Ten

LIVING LIFE TO THE FULL

I'VE ALWAYS BEEN a glass-half-full kind of person. Life is too short and too precious to be unhappy, and I try my best to cherish every moment and celebrate the good times with the people I love most. Family means the world to me – nothing else comes close – and my idea of heaven is spending quality time with my relatives . . . of whom there are plenty. Tyson and I have dozens of aunts, uncles and cousins scattered across the country and we do our very best to stay in touch with our extended family, both on the Fury side and the Mulroy side. This isn't always easy – they all have busy home lives, just like us – but making the effort to see one another, even if it's two or three times a year, is always worth it. It's good to keep close and stay connected.

Hooking up with our nearest and dearest allows us to have a good old catch-up and share all our news; there's almost always a wedding on the horizon or a baby on the way (including mine, more often than not!). It's also great for all the family's kids to intermingle because, in an ideal world, we'd like the cousins to grow up as friends, not strangers. Seeing all my nieces and nephews thriving and blossoming is lovely, although sometimes it makes you realise how quickly time flies. Those toddlers become teenagers before you know it.

'Oh wow, that *can't* be little James over there ... hasn't he shot up?' I'll say at my aunt's summer barbecue.

'He has, I know ... but look at your Prince! He's massive!' a cousin will reply. 'He'll be taller than Tyson soon!'

Marking a family milestone, whether it's a birthday, a christening or an anniversary, is always a good excuse for me to throw a big family party. I really enjoy arranging them so I can get everyone together in one place for a great time. Tyson and I aren't great lovers of VIP functions, other than post-fight parties or fundraising events. It's just not our scene. We much prefer to party with our loved ones than with people we barely know, and we certainly aren't bothered about getting snapped by the paparazzi on some red carpet or other.

I've organised some memorable celebrations through the years, including a glitzy Las Vegas-themed thirteenth-birthday bash at a local hotel for Venezuela, a glamorous pink-and-gold themed 'do' in a posh marquee to mark my mam's sixty-fifth birthday, and a surprise afternoon tea at a country pub for my sister Montana when she turned thirty-three. In the summer of 2022 I held a movie night-themed party at home to celebrate Tyson's thirty-fourth birthday, and to mark his retirement from boxing, which he'd recently announced. A few weeks later he changed his mind, however, and was soon back in the ring, fighting (and beating) Derek Chisora at Wembley Arena. This about-turn didn't come as a massive shock to me, to be honest. Even now, I have no idea when my husband will retire. All I know is that he's happy to continue fighting while he's in excellent shape and in good health. Only he will know when the time is right to finally hang up his gloves for good, although it's definitely something we'll discuss together – and then we'll have another party!

Tyson's thirty-fourth proved to be an unforgettable evening. The weather in Morecambe was beautiful, so we took full advantage by laying down a VIP red carpet outside the house – just like the Oscars – and rigging up a big inflatable screen on the front lawn, beside some comfy seats and sofas. Our guests were able to relax while watching a variety of films, which included the fantastic *Legend,* starring Tom Hardy as both Kray twins. For party food, we wheeled in some popcorn and candy-floss machines and served up burgers, hot dogs and fries

– proper, old-fashioned cinema snacks. I was so pleased with the end result, as was Tyson. It was so quirky and original. Some people said it was the best party they'd ever attended, which was lovely to hear.

All things considered, I think I'm quite a decent hostess. I'm a born organiser (I have to be, with so many kids to marshal!) and I have a pretty good eye for detail, always making sure that everything from A to Z is covered. However, I'm happy to admit that, in order to reduce the burden, I sometimes seek the help and expertise of specialist party planners. It just makes my life easier and stops me having to run around like a headless chicken. I haven't always had a helping hand, though; a few years ago, when I only had a couple of toddlers to look after, I did everything myself. I used to host their birthday parties at home, laying on traditional party games and dishing out jelly and ice cream. Little kids are easily pleased. My mam used to say, 'Just give them a balloon, a piece of cake and a party bag, Paris, and they'll be over the moon.' She wasn't wrong.

However, as my family grew larger, and their friendship group grew wider, these parties became more crazy and chaotic. Kids would run riot, drinks would be spilled, toys would be broken and I'd end up almost rocking in the corner, counting down the minutes until hometime. I reached a point where I'd had my fill, so, to make life easier (and to preserve my carpets and my sanity), I decided to hire local venues instead, like restaurants or play centres, where the kids could make as much mess as they liked, and the staff were on hand to help out whenever needed.

More recently, my favourite party planning firm has helped me create special birthday themes, depending on what current crazes my sons or daughters are into. So that might be Marvel superheroes for Adonis – he's a massive Spider-Man fan – or the *Frozen* movie for Valencia, who adores all things Disney (I can't tell you the number of times I've had to play the movie soundtrack in the car; I reckon I can sing 'Let It Go' word for word).

As their mother, it's so nice to help the kids celebrate their birthday in style. I love seeing their eyes light up on their special occasion, with all their friends and family around them. But at the same time I hope I've brought them up to realise how fortunate they are. They're very lucky to enjoy such lavish get-togethers. In all fairness, little Adonis was overflowing with gratitude after his Marvel party.

'Thank you, Mam and Dad,' he kept saying to me and Tyson, over and over again, bouncing up and down in his Spider-Man get-up. 'That was the best party *ever . . .*'

* * *

So what makes my parties go with a bang? Even before the planners set to all the fine detail, I'll have already compiled all my basic do's and don'ts. Most crucial of all for the big occasions is putting together my guest list. Good company is at the heart of any successful party, I think, so I'll invite all my favourite people, from close family members to long-time friends, who I know are going to get along well. There's nothing worse than a party with a flat and awkward atmosphere, although I can't say that's ever the case when the fun-loving Furys are around! I'm always over-generous with the invites, too, as there'll inevitably be a handful of no-shows on the night, for whatever reason. This way the room won't look sparse, and there won't be much leftover party food.

The party planners will generally look after all elements of the design and décor, based on the theme we've chosen together prior to the event. They always do such a brilliant job – their creative talents are amazing – and their input takes a lot of the weight off my shoulders. With so many kids to look after, I just don't have the time to properly organise everything from scratch. But, all that being said, I do work very closely with the team – I'm quite hands-on – and they'll always consult me and seek my advice.

It's vitally important that I cater for the right number of people, too. More is always better than less, and if I've invited 100 people I'll usually provide enough for 120. As a rule, I never lay on anything that's too fussy or fancy and usually ask the catering team to come up with a simple, easy-to-eat buffet. I much prefer this to a sit-down meal. In my experience, guests are perfectly happy with finger food like quiche Lorraine, sausage rolls and chicken drumsticks, alongside a nice variety of sand-wiches. For dessert, I'll provide platters of cakes, flans and pastries, together with sweet treats for the kids, like biscuits and mini-muffins.

I like to get the party swinging with a good DJ or a live band. The party planners tend to have lots of great contacts in their little black books to call on. There's nothing better than a medley of disco floor-fillers to get people up and dancing (although the choice of tune might depend on the age range); and I'll often request a few singalong classics to round off the night, perhaps something like 'Sweet Caroline' or 'Hotel California'. Gypsies love to belt out a tune, none more so than Tyson, but my side of the family – the Mulroy clan – are also well known for their powerful voices, particularly my dad. Sometimes these singalongs will continue long after the live band has left. There have been occasions when we've all had to be gently escorted from the premises, well into the early hours.

'We need to lock up now, if that's OK,' a member of staff will say, rattling their keys.

'Of course, no problem, we'll be on our way,' I'll reply. 'Time to call a taxi, Tyson . . .'

To say they pulled out all the stops for Venezuela's thirteenth birthday was an understatement. It was an incredible night. The venue was turned into a Las Vegas-style casino (minus the proper gambling, of course) with authentic card tables, roulette wheels and fruit machines. The place was decorated with giant dice and jumbo playing cards, and Venezuela's guests were welcomed onto the red carpet by dancing girls in feather headdresses, posing either side of a huge balloon arch. We laid on a long table of casino-themed snacks, including cupcakes with dollar signs and a magnificent three-tier birthday cake, and, throughout the evening, friends and family were entertained with various Vegas-themed variety acts. I'd never seen anything like it. It was like being transported to the MGM Grand, which has hosted many of Tyson's title fights.

Venezuela and I chose a ritzy red and gold colour scheme for the evening, which was reflected in her birthday outfit: a glittery, off-the-shoulder minidress, teamed with a golden tiara, a pair of red heels and a chiffon train. She looked very grown up, and very chic, and I felt ever so proud of her. As a mam, it's quite special to witness your gorgeous little girl blossoming into a beautiful young woman. *My daughter, officially a teenager . . . just wow*, I remember thinking to myself.

But while I love organising special events for family members, it's always nice when this is reciprocated. Being a romantic soul, Tyson loves to mark my birthday by booking a surprise meal for two in a posh restaurant, perhaps with stopover at a swanky spa hotel. In the evening, we'll get dressed up in our finery and will celebrate my milestone in the nicest way possible: by spending some rare time together, just me and him, away from the usual Morecambe mayhem. Tyson will also spoil me with birthday presents, which can range from something small like a box of Milk Tray to something a little pricier, like the latest Chanel handbag. He'll usually write a beautiful, heartfelt message in my birthday card, too.

However, during the run-up to my thirtieth birthday in December 2019, everything went a bit weird. Tyson seemed strangely uninterested in my big milestone and just changed the subject whenever I brought it up. It was so out of character, and I put it down to his mind being elsewhere. At that time, he was preparing for a huge bout in Las Vegas with world heavyweight champion Deontay Wilder, so perhaps he was more distracted than usual.

Even on the morning of my birthday, Tyson didn't appear bothered. He got up early to go training, as per usual, and didn't even leave me a card to open, let alone a present. Confused and upset, I drove into Lancaster for some retail therapy. As I walked through the city centre I bumped into a friend of mine, and when she wished me happy birthday I just burst into tears.

'It's the worst day *ever*,' I cried. 'Tyson doesn't seem interested at all, and he hasn't planned anything. I don't know what I've done wrong . . .'

'I'm sure he's got something up his sleeve, Paris,' she said, giving me a consoling hug. But I wasn't convinced.

When I returned home, Tyson was back from training. He gave me a big kiss and handed me a huge thirtieth birthday card (better late than never, I supposed). He then told me to get one of my nice outfits ready, because he'd organised a babysitter for the evening so we could go into Manchester for a quick bite to eat. Half of me felt like telling him not to bother, because it all seemed so slapdash and last-minute. *A quick bite to eat, on my big birthday?* But thank goodness I didn't. Because when I walked into my favourite city centre restaurant, I received the shock of my life. Gathered there were twenty or so of my nearest and dearest, grouped around a table festooned with balloons, sparklers, bottles of bubbly and a massive, two-tier birthday cake. Everyone yelled *'SURPRISE!'* before launching into a loud rendition of 'Happy Birthday'. And this time I cried for all the right reasons.

'You didn't think I'd organised anything, did you?' said a grinning Tyson. 'I just thought I'd surprise you, for a change.'

'I did wonder . . .' I laughed. 'But I can't believe how sneaky and secretive you've been!'

It was such a fabulous night. The venue is renowned for its brilliant live singers – they perform on a catwalk in the middle of the restaurant – and by the end of the evening I was up there too, dancing away with my girlfriends. I honestly couldn't have wished for a better start to my thirties. And it was all thanks to Tyson.

* * *

It's great to celebrate the good times in the comfort of your own home, too. Christmas in particular is a very special occasion in the Fury household. Tyson and I love taking a break from our usual schedule so we can devote more time to the kids and have lots of festive fun, whether that's decorating the tree (which is usually put up in early December), opening our presents early on Christmas morning or pulling crackers around the dining table before we tuck into turkey. But, aside from all the merry-making, I also take the religious element of Christmas very seriously. My faith is very important to me, and I will always remind the children of the Nativity message of joy, hope and celebration.

'It's not all about mince pies and Santa Claus,' I'll tell them. 'Never forget the true meaning.'

Tyson and I used to attend midnight mass every year – it's such a beautiful ceremony – but it's just not doable any more with little kids in tow. We'll say our prayers and light our candles at home instead. The house always feels really warm and inviting in December. I really like to go to town – Christmas comes but once a year! – and the place ends up looking like Santa's grotto. I don't spend a fortune on decorations, though – I find plenty of decent stuff at my local pound shop – but I love wrapping garlands round staircases, attaching wreaths to doors and dressing the fireplace and mantelpiece. Our Christmas tree fits nicely in the corner of the living room – it's an artificial one that's lasted us ages – although it's so tall I need the help of Tyson (and a ladder) to drape the tinsel, hang the baubles and pop the fairy on top.

The build-up to the big day can be pretty exhausting, though. Buying presents for my extended family is a mammoth task – I have over twenty nieces and nephews, for starters – and, more often than not, I'll find myself careering around the Trafford Centre with days to spare, buying all manner of books, games and toiletries (I like to buy actual, tangible things as opposed to just giving money). I'm often told that shopping online would make my life a whole lot easier, but that's never going to happen. As I've said before, I'm completely useless with computers, and much prefer to visit the high street in person. I get a real buzz from seeing the sparkly window displays and hearing 'Last Christmas' blaring out from every store. How could I possibly get into the festive spirit by staring at a screen?

Choosing presents for my own kids is pretty straightforward. I'm so familiar with their likes and dislikes that I have a fairly good idea of what will float their boat, whether it's a Barbie Dreamhouse for Valencia or a Minecraft backpack for Adonis. I usually buy the children a mixture of big gifts and small gifts – I get lots of bits and bobs from our local bargain stores – but I try not to go overboard. My kids aren't very demanding, to be honest, and are often just as happy to receive a selection box as they are an Xbox (and yes, like many young ones, they'll often end up playing with the boxes!). However, I think it's important that all the children are treated fairly and get the same amount of money spent on them. I don't ever want to be accused of favouritism. I don't generally encourage the little ones to write long Christmas lists to Santa, either, because I'd prefer them not to get into the habit of assuming they'll receive every item they ask for.

In contrast to the children, Tyson is extremely hard to buy for. What on earth do you get for the man who has everything? He has all the socks and underpants he could ever wish for, and has drawers brimming with accessories like belts, bucket hats and sunglasses. He doesn't have any hobbies as such – so no desire for golf clubs, snooker cues or fishing rods – and he already has plenty of boxing memorabilia displayed around the house. Tyson isn't a skincare kind of guy, either (he tends to buy his own aftershave and toiletries), and all his favourite songs and movies are streamed via the internet.

So my options are pretty limited. I can't even walk into a menswear shop and pick out a T-shirt or a pair of shorts; he's so big and broad, no item of clothing would fit him. Half the time I end up shopping online, albeit reluctantly, and will often land on the Versace website (Tyson's favourite design house). Last year I found a matching shorts-and-shirt combo in the sale, which he was delighted with. It's since become his favourite holiday outfit, so job done, Paris!

Tyson's definitely got the better half of the bargain, because I'm very easy to buy for and am not remotely fussy when it comes to presents. For me, it's the thought that counts more than anything. Tyson knows that I'm as happy with a pair of Asda pyjamas as I am with a pair of Armani jeans. And I don't expect the kids to shower me with gifts, because I think Christmas should be more geared towards them than me. Just something small and simple will do. In fact, I love it when they proudly present me with something they've made at school or nursery, like a little pressed-flower bookmark or a snowman tree decoration. Those are the sort of items that mean the most, and that I'll cherish for years to come.

On the morning of Christmas Eve, we'll usually do a few present drop-offs to our friends and family, and in the afternoon I'll get the kids looked after so Tyson and I can head off to the supermarket for the Christmas food shop. I fill a couple of trolleys with enough fresh food and store-cupboard essentials to last us through the holiday, but will always chuck in a few extra festive treats. This may include some jumbo tubs of Heroes, Celebrations, Roses and Quality Street (Crimbo isn't Crimbo without that choccy quartet!) as well as a nice selection of cheese and pâté, along with a big box of crackers to serve them with.

I'll stock up on the veg for Christmas dinner – carrots, parsnips and Brussels sprouts – although most of the meat (including the turkey) will have been pre-ordered from our local butcher. Drinks-wise, I'll load up some bottles of fizzy pop for the kids – a special treat – and might even drop a bottle of Baileys into the trolley, since that's one of my Christmas indulgences, poured over ice. More than deserved, I reckon, after such a busy year . . .

When we get back home, Tyson might take the younger kids off for a couple of hours, maybe for a brisk winter walk along the beach, which will allow me some time to complete the gift-wrapping away from prying eyes and set the table in preparation for the following day. When everyone's back home we'll enjoy some hot beef and stuffing sandwiches for tea – a Fury family tradition – after which we'll settle down on the sofa to watch a Christmas movie that we all like, perhaps *Elf* or *Home Alone*. Everyone will wear their customised festive pyjamas – another family tradition – which I get specially made, sometimes with our names embroidered on the front (we had a matching snowman theme last year). Then, before the kids' bedtime – and like millions of families across the world – we'll leave out the food plate for Father Christmas and Rudolph.

'A Penguin biscuit will do for Santa, don't you think?' I'll wink at Tyson, realising I've run out of mince pies.

'Oh, yes. That's his favourite,' he'll wink back. 'Good for his energy levels.'

Christmas Day itself is so magical when you have a houseful of hyped-up kids. Seeing everything through their eyes and experiencing their excitement just makes things extra-special. In the morning they'll wake up and rush downstairs to the living room – not too early, maybe around seven o'clock – and, after the yells of 'He's *been!*' the present-opening will commence. But while the kids rip open the wrapping paper with glee, Tyson's OCD will kick in, big style. He hates any kind of mess or untidiness, and will stand in the middle of the room holding open a black bin liner, collecting all the rubbish before it even hits the floor. It's just the way he is. I sit back and let him get on with it; it's one less job for me to do, anyway.

Once the gift exchanging is done and dusted, I'll head off to the kitchen to preheat the oven and prepare the turkey and trimmings, perhaps with a little help from the older children (especially Little Tyson, who's quite into his food, and likes to help prepare meals). I'll also put the final touches to the dining room table, decorating it with lots of streamers, sparklers and Christmas crackers and laying out my best crockery and glassware (plus plastic beakers for the accident-prone little ones!). We rarely use this room during the rest of the year, so I like to make a special effort. Nowadays, I only cook Christmas dinner for the immediate family, so more often than not it's just me, Tyson and the children sitting round the table. Other relatives, usually including my parents, my siblings and Tyson's brothers, will come over for a big buffet on Boxing Day.

As well as the Christmas turkey – usually a hefty fifteen-pounder – I'll roast another joint of meat (pork or beef, maybe) so there's plenty to go around everybody. I usually aim to serve it at one o'clock-ish, so we're finished in time for the King's speech, and so the kids have plenty of time left to play with their new toys. Christmas Day usually ends in a similar fashion to the night before, with all of us snuggling up on the sofa to watch another feel-good festive movie, happy and blessed to be together at this magnificent time of year.

*　*　*

I cherish every moment I spend with the children – particularly at Christmas-time, and during our holidays abroad – because, whether I like it or not, we won't all be under the same roof forever. The mere thought of not having my babies around is pretty hard to bear. Even now, if Prince has a sleepover at a friend's house, or Venezuela has a weekend stay at Granny's, I feel somehow incomplete, like I'm missing a body part. Time goes so fast (I can't believe how quickly they're growing up!) and I realise there'll come a day when my kids, one by one, will find a partner, fly the nest and go off to raise their own family.

Ideally by the time they reach their mid-twenties, I shall look forward to buying my first mother-of-the-bride outfit – I visualise an elegant, wide-brimmed hat! – and I know for sure I'll get really emotional on the day, as I witness my boy or girl tying the knot and beginning their new chapter. Tyson will feel exactly the same; no doubt. He'll probably be in tears when he has the honour of giving his daughters away. I know my parents were overjoyed watching me and my new husband exchanging our vows, all those years ago.

Tyson and I often wonder what the future holds for our children and, like all parents, more than anything we want them to be happy and content, and to have a solid relationship and a fulfilled family life. We can't control who they're going to fall for, of course, but we'd really like them to meet long-term partners who are kind, caring and considerate; men or women who want to get married for all the right reasons, and who love our son or daughter for who *they* are, not who their father is. I'm sure Venezuela, Prince and their siblings will be a good judge of character in that respect, but if I had my suspicions about a future partner's intentions, or was worried about my child's decision-making, I'd feel obliged to drop a few subtle hints.

But I'd imagine it would be hard for a parent to strike that balance between voicing your opinion on the one hand, and allowing your offspring to make their own choices (and maybe learn from their mistakes) on the other. In many ways, I hope my children and I will be able to mirror the relationship I enjoy with my own mother. We have such a special bond, me and Mam, and she's my first port of call whenever I require some sensible advice or guidance. She'll never lecture or patronise me, though; she'll just tell me to weigh up the situation and apply my own judgement.

'If it was me, I'd probably do it this way,' she'll say, 'but it's your call, Paris, and you have to decide what's right for you.'

And as for choosing a vocation in life, I'd like my kids to do what makes them happy, whether that's as a busy stay-at-home parent like me, or something more high profile like their dad. Both have equal merit as far as I'm concerned. But I don't fancy the idea of them floating around, doing nothing in particular. I want them to have some drive, direction and get-up-and-go, whichever path they choose. I know some parents try to map out their youngsters' futures, from kindergarten to university, but that's just not my style. I'm from the *que sera, sera* school of parenting: whatever will be, will be. I don't heap pressure on them – so no big targets or high expectations – and instead just encourage them to do their best, and focus on things they enjoy. That was essentially the advice we were given by our parents, Tyson with his boxing and me with my beauty therapy.

'You can do anything, and be anything,' Mam and Dad would say to me. 'We'll never hold you back.'

Sometimes I wonder what jobs and professions the older children will choose, now that they have their own hobbies and interests (it's far too early to tell with the toddlers, of course). Little Tyson, for instance, who loves eating out and spending time in the kitchen, and insists he's going to be a top chef (I look forward to him rustling up a sumptuous Christmas dinner in the future, so I can put my feet up for a change). Like me, Venezuela is very much into fashion and beauty – she loves putting outfits together, and experimenting with make-up – so perhaps she'll eventually want to go down that avenue.

Prince is quite sporty – he's always loved wrestling – and sometimes says he'd love to be the WWE's very own Gypsy Prince. Recently, though, he's also started to train at Tyson's boxing gym, but that's been entirely off his own bat. We've not forced him at all. Children with famous parents are sometimes expected to follow in their footsteps – whether they're an actor, a singer or an athlete – but we'd never dream of pushing our kids in one particular direction. If anything, Tyson has said he'd much rather his kids steer clear of boxing and choose another way of life, because he knows full well how hazardous the sport is. And I'd *hate* to see a child of mine in the boxing ring; it's traumatic enough watching Tyson getting punched in the face, let alone my own flesh and blood.

But as someone who's always striven to be a good wife and mother, there's one thing I'm sure about: family life should always come before your career. Don't get me wrong, I'd be delighted if any of my children became a teacher, a lawyer or a business whizz, but it's my belief that the happiest and most successful people have a decent support network already in place, back at home. Tyson has achieved so much as a boxer, of course, but he's the first to credit me and the kids for playing our part. He knows he wouldn't have hit the sporting heights without the comfort and security of a stable family life. We're like his safety net. Even when he lost his way, during his mental breakdown, it was our unconditional love that pulled him through and gave him a reason to fight on, inside and outside the boxing ring.

And Tyson loves nothing more than sharing his triumphs with the family. Bringing home his title belt soon after a big fight, is always a special moment that gets the children giddy with excitement. Their daddy is the Gypsy King and a *real-life superhero*! And I'm always so proud of him, too, of course. I know how hard he's worked, and the sacrifices he's made, to reach that summit.

'You can be the wealthiest athlete in the world, winning things left, right and centre,' Tyson will say, 'but if you've got no one to come home to, and no one to enjoy your success with, what's the point?'

I couldn't agree more. It's great to share the love.

* * *

I don't really spend too much time gazing into the future. My home life is way too crazy and chaotic for that. Put it this way, you don't get much chance for deep thought and contemplation when you've got hungry babies to feed and rowdy toddlers to amuse. Neither do I have the fortune-telling skills of my Granny Mary who, when she lived in 1970s Las Vegas, read the palms of showbiz stars including Liberace, the famously flashy pianist. She no longer does it these days, now she's in her nineties, but back then she had the celebrities queuing up for her wise words and prophecies.

However, there are times when Tyson and I, usually over a quiet dinner for two, might have some fun by imagining what our life might look like a few years down the line, when my husband has retired from boxing and the children have spread their wings. Things will probably be a little calmer, we're both agreed on that. Tyson will forever be admired as a

273

boxer, and will always have his fan base – and rightly so, considering his sporting achievements – but, over time, the spotlight on him will naturally fade. But since neither of us are fame-hungry people, that prospect rests perfectly easy with us. We've never craved celebrity, and can take it or leave it. Even the TV documentaries we appear in are not a bid for mega-stardom. Anything but. We allow cameras into our home so people can see us in our true light and form their own opinions, instead of relying on hearsay or gossip. Believe me, we'll be more than happy to take a step out of the limelight when that time comes, so we can get on with a more normal and ordinary life.

But I'm sure that, one day, Tyson and I will be able to look back at our twenties and thirties and appreciate the amazing experiences and opportunities that the world of boxing has given us. It's been so lovely to enjoy all these moments together – from Las Vegas to Los Angeles, and from London to Dusseldorf – but I think it'll be a case of 'been there, done that . . . now it's time to move on.' And while I'll never forget the drama and excitement of Tyson's fight nights, I certainly won't miss them when they're gone. As a wife, the strain and worry can be intolerable – the fear, the dread, the panic – and the prospect of my husband finally stepping out of the boxing ring, and out of harm's way, fills me with relief.

Whatever the future has in store, though, I can't ever imagine us being in a situation where it's just the two of us, sitting on the sofa in front of the TV, wearing our matching pyjamas and eating Tyson's favourite bacon pudding. We love the hustle and bustle of family life and I can't envisage us being all alone in a quiet house, even after our children have flown the nest. Our door will always be open for the kids to come and go as they please at a moment's notice, perhaps with their own families in tow. In ten years' time the Fury family might even have multiplied, God willing, with a few grandchildren on the scene. Everyone tells me how much pleasure your grand-kids can bring, so hopefully that'll be the case with me. Like my own mam, I think I'd be a devoted granny, ready and willing to help out where necessary.

'I'll babysit the children, Prince, no problem at all,' I could imagine myself saying. 'Go and have yourselves a romantic night out, just the two of you. It'll do you the world of good.'

Because that's essentially what being a Fury is all about. Putting the family first and being there for each other, no matter what. Treating our loved ones with kindness and compassion, especially in their time of need. Preserving our traditional Gypsy values, and passing them down to the next generation. And coping with family life as best we can, even though running a busy household while raising lots of kids can be a challenge and a half. But, despite all the chaos and craziness, and all the twists and turns, I wouldn't change my life for the world. Being a mam will remain my proudest honour and my greatest achievement. In years to come, when my children are grown up and my life has slowed down, I may reflect on all the nappy-changing and the sleepless nights, and all the school runs and the shopping trolleys, and ask myself one simple question.

'How *did* I do it?'

ACKNOWLEDGEMENTS

To my great team at Hodder – especially Rowena Webb, Rebecca Mundy, Alasdair Oliver, Kate Brunt and Christian Duck – who did such a great job with my first book, *Love & Fury*, that they encouraged me to believe this book will be every bit as much loved. My thanks too to Joanne Lake for all the conversations and help in putting this one together. And to Lesley Hodgson for helping with the pictures.

PICTURE ACKNOWLEDGEMENTS

Inset 1

All author's own

Inset 2

Page 1, top left: © The Mega Agency

Page 1, bottom left: © Backgrid

Page 5, middle left: © Julian Finney/Getty Images

Page 6, middle left: © Splash by Shutterstock

Other images all author's own